This monograph is a greatly expanded and updated version of the series of lectures that Joseph Traub presented by invitation of the Accademia Nazionale dei Lincei at the Scuola Normale Superiore in Pisa. Arthur Werschulz has joined him as co-author.

The twin themes of computational complexity and information pervade this book. It starts with an introduction to information-based complexity, that is, the computational complexity of continuous mathematical models. It then moves to a variety of topics, including breaking the curse of dimensionality, complexity of path integration, solvability of ill-posed problems, value of information in computation, assigning values to mathematical hypotheses, and mathematical finance.

The style is informal, and the goal is motivation and insight. Precise statements and proofs can be found in the monographs and papers included in the comprehensive bibliography. The book will be essential reading for researchers in the many disciplines influenced by the computational complexity of continuous problems. Because of its expository style, the book will be welcomed by beginning graduate students and advanced undergraduates.

COMPLEXITY AND INFORMATION

COMPLEXITY AND INFORMATION

J. F. TRAUB

Department of Computer Science, Columbia University
External Professor, Santa Fe Institute

A. G. WERSCHULZ

Department of Computer and Information Science, Fordham University
Department of Computer Science, Columbia University

CAMBRIDGE
UNIVERSITY PRESS

PUBLISHED BY THE PRESS SYNDICATE OF THE UNIVERSITY OF CAMBRIDGE
The Pitt Building, Trumpington Street, Cambridge, United Kingdom

CAMBRIDGE UNIVERSITY PRESS
The Edinburgh Building, Cambridge CB2 2RU, UK http://www.cup.cam.ac.uk
40 West 20th Street, New York, NY 10011-4211, USA http://www.cup.org
10 Stamford Road, Oakleigh, Melbourne 3166, Australia

First published 1998

Printed in the United Kingdom at the University Press, Cambridge

Typeset in Computer Modern 10/13pt, in TEX

A catalogue record of this book is available from the British Library

Library of Congress cataloguing in publication data

Traub, J. F. (Joseph Frederick), 1932–
Complexity and information / J.F. Traub, A.G. Werschulz.
p. cm.
Includes bibliographical references and index.
ISBN 0 521 48005 1 (hardback)
1. Computational complexity. I. Werschulz, Arthur G. II. Title.
QA267.7.T7 1998
511.3–dc21 98-29464 CIP

ISBN 0 521 48005 1 hardback
ISBN 0 521 48506 1 paperback

To my friend, companion, and wife
Pamela McCorduck
—JFT

ב"ה

To my children
Aaron and Nathaniel
תו.ש.ל.ב.ע.
—AGW

To our friend and colleague
Henryk Woźniakowski
—JFT & AGW

Contents

Preface

This book is a greatly expanded and updated version of the series of
lectures that Joseph Traub presented by invitation of the Accademia
Nazionale dei Lincei at the Scuola Normale Superiore in Pisa, in May
and June, 1993. Arthur Werschulz has joined him as co-author.

The book consists of three parts. Part One is a self-contained exposition of the field of information-based complexity (IBC), which studies
the computational complexity of problems for which the available information is partial, contaminated, and priced. In particular, it studies
the computational complexity of continuous models that are typical of
many scientific and engineering disciplines. Part Two is a selection of
topics that are of particular interest to the authors, and hopefully to the
readers. It reflects a bias towards work done at Columbia University,
and does not try to cover the world-wide research in IBC. Furthermore,
topics are included that are not directly within the realm of IBC and
its applications. Part Three contains a bibliography of over 400 recent
books and papers, which will suggest further reading on the material
covered in Parts One and Two and will provide pointers to IBC research
not covered in this book.

The style of this monograph is informal. There are few formal statements of theorems and no proofs. The goal is motivation and insight;
precise statements and proofs may be found in other monographs and
papers.

We are grateful to the following for their careful reading of the manu-
script and for suggesting many corrections and improvements: J. Casti,
X. Gabaix, S. Heinrich, A. Iserles, E. Novak, E. Packel, L. Plaskota,
K. Ritter, G. Wasilkowski, H. Woźniakowski. We also thank O. Patash-
nik for answering questions about the BIBTeX style file for this book.
Finally, we thank P. Jackson, our copyeditor at Cambridge University

Press, for his exemplary work; any remaining errors are the responsibility of the authors.

Joseph Traub wishes to thank the Accademia Nazionale dei Lincei for inviting him to give the Lezioni Lincee, as well as the IBM Foundation of Italy, which made the lectures possible. He thanks Professor Luigi Radicati for arranging the lectures at the Scuola Normale Superiore in Pisa and Professor Bruno Codenotti, Istituto di Matematica Computazionale del CNR, for being a wonderful scientific and personal host in Pisa. Both authors thank the National Science Foundation for grant support and JFT also wishes to thank the Alfred P. Sloan Foundation; this support made the writing of this book possible.

Columbia University
1998

Part One

Fundamentals

1

Introduction

Two themes pervade this book. They are *computational complexity* and *information*, and we will discuss them in turn.

Computational complexity is a measure of the intrinsic computational resources required to solve a mathematically posed problem. It is an *invariant*, since the computational complexity depends only on the problem, and is independent of the particular algorithm used to solve it. Just as the study of invariants is central to physics and mathematics, computational complexity is a fundamental invariant of computer science. Borrowing another analogy from physics, Packel & Traub [1987] refer to computational complexity as the *thermodynamics of computation*. Indeed, classical thermodynamics sets intrinsic limits on what any heat engine can do; these limits can be used as benchmarks for a particular engine. Similarly, computational complexity tells us the minimal resources needed to solve a problem; we can then use these limits to evaluate how close a particular algorithm comes to achieving this minimum.

"Complexity" is a word with rich connotations, and used in many ways, both formally and informally. Lloyd [1996] identified over thirty ways in which complexity is used, often modified by an adjective. Not on Lloyd's list are other senses in which complexity is used, such as a complexity measure introduced by G. D. Birkhoff [1933] in his work on the mathematics of aesthetics. Notions of complexity have also appeared in writing about the arts. Arnheim [1971] writes elegantly about visual art, citing what he calls "a need for complexity." Since the only flavor we'll encounter in this monograph is computational complexity, we'll call it "complexity" for brevity.

Our second theme is *information*. We use "information" in the everyday sense of the word, as meaning what we know about a phenomenon

3

or a problem. For the problems we'll discuss, the information will be
partial. That is, the information does not uniquely identify a physical state or an instance of a mathematical problem. Furthermore, the
information is *contaminated* with error.

Problems with partial and/or contaminated information abound in
science and in computation. Here are examples of such problems.

In weather prediction, we would like to know the current state of the
weather. Measurements are made by earth stations, planes, ships, and
satellites. Since the number of measurements is finite, the information
is partial. Inevitably, these measurements are contaminated with errors.
Hence we can only know the current weather to within some error. Since
weather appears to be chaotic, this error is amplified, and limits our
ability to forecast the weather to only a matter of days.

As a second example, we consider a computational model of the human
visual system (Marr [1981]). We give a simplified description of a small
portion of Marr's model. Imagine we are looking at a car hood. How
do we infer the shape of the hood? A depth value is the subjective
distance to a point on an object, as perceived by the viewer. The model
assumes that binocularity (or other means) yields a finite number of
depth values. Between any pair of depth values, the hood could have
any shape. However, the visual system uses the assumption that the
hood is smooth, and therefore cannot change too much between depth
values. Knowing the finite number of depth values and the smoothness
of the surface, the visual system determines the shape approximately.

Note that there are two kinds of information being used by the visual
system in this example. There is a finite number of depth values. If we
had only this partial information, the error in approximating the surface
between these depth values could be arbitrarily large. This is avoided
by the smoothness assumption. The smoothness assumption defines a
class of surfaces. We call this *global information*. Assume that the global
information is fixed for all the hoods we'll see. The depth values, which
we'll call *local information*, then limit us to a set of indistinguishable
surfaces. There are an infinite number of such surfaces, but, provided
there are enough depth values, the approximation error will be small.
Because the global information is typically fixed, we will focus on the
local information, which we'll simply call the *information*.

Our final example regarding information is a mathematical problem
that occurs in numerous disciplines. Consider a continuous (as opposed
to discrete) dynamical system. It consists of an equation that determines
how the system evolves over time and an initial condition. Assume that

the equation depends on coefficients that are real functions of a real variable. Since a digital computer can store only a finite set of numbers, these functions must be replaced by such finite sets (by, for example, evaluating these functions at a finite number of points). Therefore we have only partial information about the equation of evolution and the initial condition. Furthermore, the function values will be contaminated by round-off error.

Therefore we can, at best, hope for only an approximation to the solution of the dynamical system. To guarantee a small approximation error, we must assume global information about the initial condition and the coefficients of the evolution equation and obtain sufficient local information.

These three examples illustrate that often the information is partial and contaminated. There is *intrinsic uncertainty*, due to partial and/or contaminated information. At best, we can guarantee only an approximate solution.

There is a third important property of information—its cost. For example, taking weather measurements is a very expensive process. Evaluating functions, especially multivariate functions, can also be expensive. Therefore, we assume that information is *priced*.

Information-based complexity (IBC) is the branch of computational complexity that studies problems for which the information is partial, contaminated, and priced.

Here is a selection of the questions we'll address, and in some cases answer, in this book.

(i) What is the intrinsic uncertainty in the solution due to the available information?

(ii) How much information is needed to limit the uncertainty to a specified level?

(iii) What is the optimal information?

(iv) What is the complexity (minimal cost) of solving a problem for a given level of uncertainty?

(v) What is the optimal algorithm for solving a given problem? (An algorithm is *optimal* if it uses the information to produce an acceptable approximation to the answer at minimal cost.)

The first three questions have to do with the quantity and quality of information. They concern intrinsic uncertainty due to the available information, the amount of information needed to achieve specified un-

certainty, and optimal information. These questions are posed at the
information level.

We can answer these questions because there is a quantity, called the
radius of information, that measures the intrinsic uncertainty in the
solution due to the available information. That is, we can compute an
ε-approximation to the solution if and only if the radius of information
is at most ε.

We can consider uncertainty in various settings. In the *worst case
setting*, we guarantee an answer with error at most ε. In the *average
case setting* we give the weaker guarantee that the *expected* error is at
most ε. Many other settings are studied in IBC. In every setting, a radius
of information can be defined to measure the intrinsic uncertainty in that
setting.

As we will see in Chapter 2, arguments at the information level permit us to obtain bounds, often tight, on the computational complexity
of many problems. This may be contrasted with the situation in combinatorial complexity, where the information is complete and exact, see
Section 5 of Traub & Woźniakowski [1991a]. Because the information is
complete and exact, there is no intrinsic uncertainty in the solution, the
radius of information is always zero, and there are no information level
adversary arguments. The computational complexity of combinatorial
problems such as the traveling salesman problem is unknown. There are
only hierarchical results and the conjecture that the hierarchy does not
collapse, an example being the great open conjecture that P $\neq$ NP.

We return to IBC in general. The theory is developed over abstract
linear spaces; see Traub & Woźniakowski [1980] and Traub *et al.* [1988].
In this monograph, the emphasis will be on applications, where results
on multivariate problems often take center stage.

We regard IBC as a foundational subject, and make as few assumptions as possible. We might assume, for example, that the problem is
specified by a linear operator and that the information consists of linear
functionals. Everything else is a consequence of the theory. We hope this
gives the subject both generality and simplicity, leading to unity across
a great variety of different applications, some of which are described in
this book.

We briefly summarize what we'll cover in this monograph. Part One
is an introduction to IBC.

In Chapter 2, we introduce the basic concepts. The general formulation is given in abstract linear spaces, with scalar numerical integration
used as a simple model problem.

The applications of IBC often involve multivariate functions, sometimes of very high dimension. In the worst case deterministic setting, many problems are intractable, i.e., the complexity of many problems grows exponentially with dimension. This is sometimes called the "curse of dimensionality." Attempting to break this curse by settling for a stochastic assurance has proven to be one of the richest areas of IBC; we provide a survey of recent progress, as well as open problems, in Chapter 3.

Part Two is a selection of topics that are of particular interest to the authors.

In Chapter 4, we consider the currently very active area of rapid computation of the high-dimensional integrals that occur in mathematical finance. Since we typically encounter problems whose dimension is several hundred, the Monte Carlo (MC) algorithm, whose stochastic convergence rate is proportional to $n^{-1/2}$, has been widely used. It was believed that quasi-Monte Carlo (QMC) algorithms would not be effective for such high-dimensional integration. Surprisingly, tests on integrals from mathematical finance showed that QMC consistently beats MC by wide margins. It is an open problem to characterize classes of integrands for which QMC is superior to MC. Sloan & Woźniakowski [1998b] is an important step towards solving this problem.

In Chapter 5, we report on the work of Wasilkowski and Woźniakowski on the complexity of path integration, that is, integration over an infinite number of variables. This problem is usually solved with Monte Carlo; can it be solved with a worst case assurance? The answer depends on the smoothness of the integrands. If the integrands have finite regularity, the problem is intractable in the worst case setting. However, if the integrands are entire, then the problem is easy, even in the worst case.

In Chapter 6, we discuss the computation of ill-posed problems, reporting results found in Werschulz [1987b] and in Sections 6.7 and 7.5 of Werschulz [1991]. On the one hand, ill-posed problems are unsolvable in the worst case setting. On the other hand, every linear ill-posed problem is solvable, on the average, for all Gaussian measures. This latter result concerning the average case setting draws on a key lemma proved in Kon *et al.* [1991] and in Vakhania [1991]. Note that even though ill-posed problems are solvable in the average case setting, they can still be intractable on the average.

Much of IBC research to date deals with problems defined by linear operators. However, many of the most important problems of computation are nonlinear. In Chapter 7, we discuss complexity results for several nonlinear problems..

A central dogma of computer science is that the Turing machine is *the* appropriate abstraction of a computer. In Chapter 8, we compare and contrast the Turing machine with the real-number model as the appropriate model of computation for scientific problems.

Starting with the seminal papers of Gödel [1931] and Turing [1937], this century has witnessed a stream of impossibility theorems, including *undecidability, non-computability,* and *intractability.* In Chapter 9, we pose open questions on whether theorems from formal models limit scientific knowledge.

In Chapter 10, we use the complexity of linear programming (LP) to illustrate the dependence of complexity results on the model of computation. In 1979, Khachian analyzed an ellipsoid algorithm for LP, and showed that its cost was tractable in the Turing machine model. Then in 1982, Traub and Woźniakowski showed that the cost of the ellipsoid algorithm is not tractable in the real-number model, and conjectured that LP is not tractable in the real-number model. This conjecture is still open.

The primary focus of IBC has been on the complexity of computing approximate solutions. In Chapters 11 and 12, we discuss two new areas of investigation: the complexity of *verification* and of *implementation testing.* In verification, we are given a problem and a proposed answer, and we are asked to check whether the proposed answer is within ε of the true answer. Intuition suggests that verification is surely easier than computing. In Chapter 11, we'll see that this intuition is incorrect.

In implementation testing, we are given a specification and an implementation, such as a chip or a program. We wish to perform a finite number of tests and determine whether the implementation "conforms" to the specification. In Chapter 12, we summarize recent work on implementation testing.

Recall that we defined IBC as the branch of computational complexity that deals with problems for which the information is partial, contaminated, and priced. Although virtually any information that is available in practice will be noisy, the theory for noisy information has been less well-developed than that for exact partial information, because it is technically very difficult. Recently, Plaskota [1996c] has written an authoritative monograph on what's been accomplished, as well as much new material. In Chapter 13, we give a brief introduction to the important topic of noisy information and provide a number of applications.

In Chapter 14 we discuss an IBC-based measure of the value of information. In some important cases, this measure agrees with the mutual information as obtained from the continuous analogue of Shannon entropy. In other cases, however, the two measures disagree.

In Chapter 15, we describe the idea that since complexity is an intrinsic property of a problem, any change in complexity that stems from hypothesis H_1 rather than hypothesis H_2 is solely due to the change in hypothesis; this permits us to assign values to the hypotheses. A number of application areas illustrate the idea.

In Chapter 16, we list the open problems mentioned in the text, while in Chapter 17, we provide a brief history of IBC.

Part Three contains a bibliography of over 400 papers and books published since 1987. This is preceded by a listing of other bibliographies, which is found in Chapter 18.

2

Information-Based Complexity

In this chapter, we briefly present the main concepts of information-based complexity (IBC). A more detailed expository account may be found in Traub & Woźniakowski [1991a]. Readers who are more interested in technical details and proofs should read Traub *et al.* [1988].

We will use numerical integration as a running example in this chapter, to introduce and illustrate these concepts. The integration problem has been studied for decades. In this chapter, we will restrict our attention to univariate integration. See Chapter 3 for multivariate integration, Chapter 4 for very high-dimensional integration, and Chapter 5 for path integration. Despite the apparent simplicity of univariate integration, it is sufficiently rich to allow us to introduce a number of the important concepts of IBC.

Remark: The reader should not be misled into thinking that IBC is only about problems as simple as integration! IBC has successfully dealt with approximation, ill-posed problems, ordinary and partial differential equations, integral equations, and general multivariate problems. See Novak [1988a], Plaskota [1996c], Traub *et al.* [1988], and Werschulz [1991] for particulars. □

2.1 An Example: Integration

We wish to compute integrals

$$\int_0^1 f(x)\,dx$$

of functions f over the unit interval. Most functions arising in practice do not have antiderivatives expressible as a finite combination of elementary functions, and so one cannot utilize the fundamental theorem of calculus to compute the integral exactly. Hence we have to solve the problem numerically.

What do we know about the functions f that we are integrating? Typically, we assume that we know

$$N(f) = [f(t_1), \ldots, f(t_n)],$$

the values of f at a finite set of points in $[0, 1]$. These sample points $t_1, \ldots, t_n$ may be specified in one of two ways:

- *adaptively:* That is, a particular sample point may depend on the previously sampled information, i.e., $t_i = t_i(f(t_1), \ldots, f(t_{i-1}))$. Furthermore, the total number n of sample points may also be chosen adaptively, so that $n = n(f)$, allowing arbitrary termination criteria.
- *nonadaptively:* That is, the number n and locations $t_1, \ldots, t_n$ of the sample points are the same for all integrands f.

Clearly adaptive information is inherently sequential, whereas nonadaptive information may (at least in principle) be evaluated in parallel.

These function values are now used as input to a combinatory algorithm, which produces a result of the form

$$\int_0^1 f(x) \, dx \approx U(f) := \phi\big(f(t_1), \ldots, f(t_n)\big),$$

where ϕ is a mapping whose input is a finite set of numbers.

Let us call the information $N(f)$ *local* information, since it depends on the integrand f. Local information is not strong enough to allow us to solve our problem—if we only know the value of a function at a finite set $\{t_1, \ldots, t_n\}$ of points, its integral could be *any* real number!†

Hence, we cannot conclude anything about an integral if we have only local information about the integrand. We also need *global* information, which restricts the class of integrands to a particular class F of functions.

---

† Indeed, for any function f, consider the "fooling function"

$$\tilde{f}_\kappa(x) = f(x) + \kappa \prod_{i=1}^n (x - t_i)^2,$$

where κ is an arbitrary positive number. Then $\tilde{f}_\kappa(t_i) = f(t_i)$ for $1 \le i \le n$, so that $N(\tilde{f}_\kappa) = N(f)$, and hence no algorithm using N can distinguish between f and $\tilde{f}_\kappa$. But by making an appropriate choice of κ, we can make $\int_0^1 \tilde{f}_\kappa(x) \, dx$ take on any value. In other words, if our only information about the integrand f is $N(f)$, an adversary could tell us (after our painstakingly chosen algorithm produces an approximation to $\int_0^1 f(x) \, dx$) that the integrand was "really" $\tilde{f}_\kappa$. Since κ can be chosen arbitrarily, the worst case error of our approximation is infinite.

In this chapter, we will use a simple (but typical) integrand class F consisting of functions f satisfying

$$|f(\xi) - f(\eta)| \leq L\,|\xi - \eta| \qquad \forall\, \xi, \eta \in [0,1]. \tag{2.1}$$

That is, the integrands are Lipschitz continuous, and we know an upper bound L on the Lipschitz constant

$$\mathrm{Lip}(f) = \max_{\xi,\eta \in [0,1]} \frac{|f(\xi) - f(\eta)|}{|\xi - \eta|}.$$

Remark: We briefly discuss the restriction (2.1) that defines our integrand class F. There are two aspects of this condition. The first is knowledge about the smoothness of f, i.e., that f satisfies a Lipschitz condition. The second is that we know a uniform bound L on $\mathrm{Lip}(f)$.

Suppose we have no such bound, but we do know that f satisfies a Lipschitz condition. If we only know the value of f at a finite set of points, the integral of f can be any real number. This cannot be fixed by increasing the continuity of f, i.e., by requiring that f have a certain number of derivatives.† Thus we cannot solve the problem if we only know the smoothness of f.

Alternatively, we might ask what happens if f is only continuous, but we have a bound on f, say $|f(x)| \leq L$ for $x \in [0,1]$. We then find that the integral of f can be any number between $-L$ and L, regardless of the number of evaluation points.‡ So we cannot solve the problem if we only have a bound on the function.   □

For a particular integrand f, how can we best make use of the function values $y = N(f)$? Recall that we require the Lipschitz constant to be at most L. It is easy to see that an envelope for the set of all integrands $\tilde{f}$ for which $N(\tilde{f}) = y$ is given by piecewise linear functions with slope $\pm L$. Moreover, if we let f_{upper} and f_{lower} denote the upper and lower functions that determine the envelope, then $f_{\mathrm{mid}} = \frac{1}{2}(f_{\mathrm{upper}} + f_{\mathrm{lower}})$ is the func-

---

† An adversary can trick us by using the same fooling function $\tilde{f}_\kappa$ as was used previously.

‡ Indeed, choose $\ell \in [-L, L]$, let $f \in F$, and pick a set $\{t_1, \ldots, t_n\}$ of sample points. For small $\delta > 0$, our adversary can produce a fooling function $\tilde{f}_{\ell,\delta}$ as a piecewise-linear function satisfying

$$\tilde{f}_{\ell,\delta}(x) = \begin{cases} f(t_i) & \text{if } x = t_i \text{ for some } i \in \{1, \ldots, n\}, \\ \ell & \text{if } \mathrm{dist}(x, \{t_1, \ldots, t_n\}) \geq \delta. \end{cases}$$

Then $\tilde{f}_{\ell,\delta}$ belongs to the integrand class and $N(\tilde{f}_{\ell,\delta}) = N(f)$, yet by choosing sufficiently small δ, we can make $\int_0^1 \tilde{f}_{\ell,\delta}(x)\,dx$ arbitrarily close to ℓ.

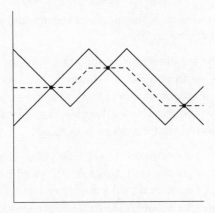

Fig. 2.1 Functions sharing the same information

tion whose maximal distance from any other function in the envelope is
minimal. (This is illustrated for the case $L = 1$ in Figure 2.1.)

Let $\phi^*(y) = \int_0^1 f_{\text{mid}}(x)\, dx$. Then $g = \phi^*(y)$ minimizes

$$\sup_{\tilde{f}} \left| g - \int_0^1 \tilde{f}(x)\, dx \right|,$$

the supremum being taken over all integrands $\tilde{f} \in F$ for which $N(\tilde{f}) = y$.
Hence $\phi^*(y)$ is the best possible estimate of $\int_0^1 f(x)\, dx$ over all integrands
yielding the sample values y.

We wish to obtain an explicit formula for ϕ^*. Without loss of generality, suppose that $0 \le t_1 < t_2 < \ldots < t_n \le 1$. Let f_{pwlin} be the piecewise
linear interpolant of the points $(0, y_1), (t_1, y_1), \ldots, (t_n, y_n), (1, y_n).$† It is
geometrically clear that

$$\int_0^1 f_{\text{mid}}(x)\, dx = \int_0^1 f_{\text{pwlin}}(x)\, dx,$$

and so

$$\phi^*(y) = y_1 t_1 + \sum_{i=1}^{n-1} \tfrac{1}{2}(y_i + y_{i+1})(t_{i+1} - t_i) + y_n(1 - t_n). \qquad (2.2)$$

Moreover, it is easy to see that this algorithm is a composite trapezoidal
rule, with endpoint modifications if $t_1 > 0$ or $t_n < 1$. In short, this
modified trapezoidal rule is an optimal algorithm for integration in the

---

† Note that we add the two extra points $(0, y_1)$ and $(1, y_n)$, and we define f_{pwlin} to
be constant on the subintervals $[0, t_1]$ and $[t_n, 1]$. We have $f_{\text{mid}} = f_{\text{pwlin}}$ on $[0, t_1]$
and $[t_n, 1]$.

class F. (For other classes F the modified trapezoidal rule will generally not be an optimal algorithm.)

Remark: Note that we allow *any* combination (not necessarily linear) of the sample values as an algorithm. However, the modified trapezoidal rule $\phi^*(y)$ is a linear combination of the sample values $y_1, \ldots, y_n$. Hence, although arbitrary algorithms are allowable, we were able to prove that a linear combination of sample values is optimal.   □

We examine this process more closely. Suppose that i_{m} is a mathematical input, i.e., a particular integrand. We would like to obtain the exact solution o_{m} (a mathematical output) of the integration problem by applying the integration operator to the mathematical input i_{m}. But a computational algorithm cannot use the mathematical input i_{m}; it can only use an input i_{c} consisting of a finite set of numbers. Since a real function of a real variable on $[0, 1]$ is not uniquely determined by a finite set of sample values, there will exist different mathematical inputs yielding the same computational input. Thus the *information operator* mapping the mathematical input i_{m} to the computational output i_{c} is many-to-one.

Since the computational input does not uniquely determine the mathematical input, it follows that no matter how an algorithm is chosen, in general there will exist mathematical inputs i_{m} for which $o_{\mathrm{c}} \neq o_{\mathrm{m}}$.

2.2 A General Formulation of IBC

We now present a general formulation of information-based complexity. Let

$$S: F \to G$$

be a *solution operator*. Here, G is a normed linear space and F is a subset of a normed linear space. We wish to compute an approximation to $S(f)$ for an arbitrary *problem element* $f \in F$.

Recall that in Chapter 1, we said that we have both *global* and *local* *information* about our problem. The global information is specified by F, which captures our a priori knowledge of the problem elements (for instance, smoothness, convexity, etc.). Since the global information often remains fixed, we call the local information the *information*. The information we have about a problem element $f \in F$ is obtained by computing a finite set

$$N(f) = [L_1(f), \ldots, L_n(f)] \tag{2.3}$$

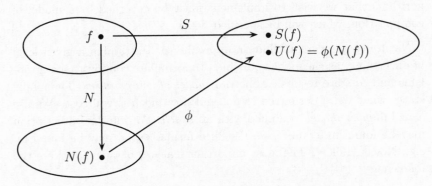

Fig. 2.2 Information-based computation

of functionals of f. Here, $L_1, \ldots, L_n \in \Lambda$, where Λ is a given class of *permissible information functionals*. These functionals are often, but not always, linear. We say that N is an *information operator*. As illustrated by the integration problem, the functionals $L_1, \ldots, L_n$ may be chosen either adaptively or nonadaptively; furthermore, $n = n(f)$ may also be chosen adaptively. If either the L_i or n are chosen adaptively, we say the information N is *adaptive*.

The computational input $N(f)$ consists of a finite set of numbers, whereas the mathematical input f generally lives in an infinite-dimensional space. Thus the information operator N is many-to-one, i.e., we only have *partial information* about our problem elements. This means that no matter how clever we are, in general we can never design an algorithm that gives the exact answer for all problem elements. By an (idealized) *algorithm*, we mean any mapping

$$\phi : N(F) \to G.$$

For any $f \in F$, we obtain an approximation $U(f)$ to $S(f)$ by

$$U(f) = \phi(N(f)).$$

These ideas are illustrated in Figure 2.2.

Remark: The decomposition $U = \phi \circ N$ of the approximation operator U is crucial to IBC. It permits analysis at the information level. □

Remark: The reader familiar with the usual definition of algorithm may be surprised by the generality of our definition of an (idealized) algorithm as an arbitrary mapping from $N(F)$ to G. The advantage of this approach is that it strengthens any negative results. Of course, any algorithms that we wish to implement must be governed by a model of computation, which will be specified below.   □

Naturally, we want to find an approximation attaining a given level of uncertainty as cheaply as possible. To formulate computational problems and to state results, we need a *model of computation*. The model states what we're permitted to do, and how much it will cost. We use a *real-number model*, equipped with an *oracle*. An informal description may be found in Traub *et al.* [1988]; a formalization may be found in, e.g., Novak [1995c]. The most important features of this model are the following:

- We are charged for each information operation. That is, for any $f \in F$ and any $L \in \Lambda$, the cost of computing $L(f)$ is c. We assume that this cost c is independent of f and L.
- Let Ω denote the set of permissible *combinatory* (or *arithmetic*) *operations*. This includes vector space operations in G (addition and scalar multiplication) as well as operations in $\mathbb{R}$ (such as arithmetic operations, comparisons, and perhaps certain elementary function evaluations). Unless stated otherwise, we shall assume that each operation in Ω is performed exactly with unit cost.

Note that it is reasonable to assume that $c \geq 1$, i.e., that an information operation should cost at least as much as a combinatory operation. Indeed, since one would expect an information operation to cost much more than a combinatory operation, it is reasonable to suppose that $c \gg 1$.

Remark: The model of computation in discrete computational complexity is typically given by a Turing machine.. We compare computation over the reals with the Turing machine model in Chapter 9.   □

The error and cost of computing an approximation $U(f) = \phi(N(f))$ for any fixed $f \in F$ are defined very simply. The error is

$$e(U, f) = \|S(f) - U(f)\|.$$

The cost is the sum of the cost of obtaining the information and the cost of combining this information. That is,

$$\text{cost}(U, f) = \text{cost}(N, f) + \text{cost}(\phi, N(f)).$$

Here $\text{cost}(N, f)$ denotes the *information cost* of computing the information $y = N(f)$. For N of the form (2.3), $\text{cost}(N, f) \geq c\, n(f)$. (Note that this is an equality when N is nonadaptive. However, for adaptive information, we may have to account for the possible cost of determining the functionals comprising $N(f)$ for a particular $f \in F$.) The *combinatory cost*, $\mathrm{cost}(\phi, N(f))$, is the number of combinatory operations from Ω used when computing $U(f) = \phi(y)$.

We've now defined error and cost for a fixed element f. But computational complexity is only interesting for a set (often infinite) of input elements. Here, we will define the *worst case* setting. This is the most conservative setting, providing the strongest assurance to the user. The *randomized* (Monte Carlo) and *average case* settings will be defined in Chapter 3; the *probabilistic* setting will be defined in Chapter 11.

The definitions of error and cost in the worst case setting are very natural:

$$e(U) \equiv e^{\mathrm{wor}}(U) := \sup_{f \in F} e(U, f),$$
$$\mathrm{cost}(U) \equiv \mathrm{cost}^{\mathrm{wor}}(U) := \sup_{f \in F} \mathrm{cost}(U, f).$$

We call U an ε-*approximation* if $e(U) \leq \varepsilon$. We want to compute an ε-approximation as cheaply as possible. The *computational complexity* of a problem is

$$\mathrm{comp}(\varepsilon) = \inf\{\, \mathrm{cost}(U) : U \text{ such that } e(U) \leq \varepsilon \,\}. \tag{2.4}$$

If

$$e(U) \leq \varepsilon \qquad \text{and} \qquad \mathrm{cost}(U) = \mathrm{comp}(\varepsilon)$$

for an approximation U given by information N and an algorithm ϕ, then ϕ is said to be an *optimal algorithm* and N is said to be *optimal information*. Note that since the infimum of the empty set is conventionally taken to be infinite, we find that $\mathrm{comp}(\varepsilon) = \infty$ if the set on the right-hand side of (2.4) is empty, i.e., if we cannot compute an ε-approximation.

Remark: The complexity depends on a number of parameters (such as the solution operator S, the problem elements F, the permissible information operators Λ, the permissible combinatory operations Ω) in addition to the error ε. Whenever it is important to do so, we will show this dependence explicitly. For example, the complexity of a multidimensional problem may depend on the dimension d, so we write $\mathrm{comp}(\varepsilon, d)$.

$\square$

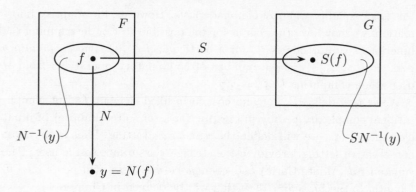

Fig. 2.3 Problem elements sharing the same information

Remark: The worst case setting is sometimes called the minimax setting, since we are minimizing the maximum error and cost. □

We can now state two of the goals of IBC:

- Determine the complexity of a given problem in various settings.
- Find an optimal (or nearly optimal) algorithm and information for computing an ε-approximation.

At first glance, this might seem to be a daunting task, since we apparently would need to consider every algorithm that computes an ε-approximation, and then to select the one with minimal cost.

We use an indirect approach to achieving these goals, which is based on finding the uncertainty inherent in using a given amount of information. This will allow us to determine the "information complexity," i.e., the minimal cost of calculating the information needed for an ε-approximation. For many important problems, the information complexity is close to the problem complexity.

We continue to confine ourselves to the worst case setting. Let N be an information operator. For $f \in F$, let $y = N(f)$. Then

$$N^{-1}(y) = \{\, \tilde{f} \in F : N(\tilde{f}) = y \,\}$$

is the set of all indistinguishable problem elements, having the same information as f. Similarly, $SN^{-1}(y)$ is the set of indistinguishable solution elements, see Figure 2.3.

Recalling that the radius of a set is the radius of the smallest ball containing that set, we define the *radius of information* as

$$r(N) \equiv r^{\mathrm{wor}}(N) := \sup_{y \in N(F)} \mathrm{radius}\left(SN^{-1}(y)\right).$$

It is easy to check that

$$r^{\mathrm{wor}}(N) = \inf_{\phi} e^{\mathrm{wor}}(\phi, N). \qquad (2.5)$$

A proof may be found on p. 44 of Traub & Woźniakowski [1980].

The radius of information is defined in all settings and is one of the most basic concepts of IBC, since it measures the intrinsic uncertainty of solving the problem using given information. We can compute an ε-approximation iff $r(N) \leq \varepsilon$, modulo a technical assumption that the infimum in (2.5) is attained. Note that the radius depends only on the problem being solved and the information available for its solution. It does *not* depend on any particular algorithm using that information.

We are now able to describe (for any setting) the relation between radius of information and computational complexity for problems where the combinatory complexity is dominated by the information complexity. Here the *information complexity* and the *combinatory complexity* are the minimal information and combinatory costs of calculating an ε-approximation, respectively. Alternatively, the information (respectively, combinatory) complexity can be defined as the complexity if combinatory (respectively, information) operations are free.

We first give a lower bound on the complexity. For information N, let card(N) denote its *cardinality*, i.e., the number of functionals making up N. Let

$$m(\varepsilon) = \inf\{\, \mathrm{card}(N) : \text{information } N \text{ such that } r(N) \leq \varepsilon \,\}$$

denote the *cardinality number*. Thus any algorithm that calculates an ε-approximation must use at least $m(\varepsilon)$ information evaluations, each costing c, and so

$$\mathrm{comp}(\varepsilon) \geq c\,m(\varepsilon).$$

We now seek a matching upper bound, i.e., we wish to find an ε-approximation $U_{\varepsilon} = (\phi_{\varepsilon}, N_{\varepsilon})$ having cost close to $c\,m(\varepsilon)$. Suppose we can find information N_{ε} of cardinality $m(\varepsilon)$ whose information cost is $c\,m(\varepsilon)$ and whose radius is at most ε. Then the information complexity is $c\,m(\varepsilon)$.

Moreover, suppose that there exists an approximation $U_{\varepsilon} = (\phi_{\varepsilon}, N_{\varepsilon})$

for which

$$e(U_\varepsilon) \leq \varepsilon$$

and

$$\text{cost}(\phi_\varepsilon, N_\varepsilon(f)) \ll c\,m(\varepsilon) \qquad \forall f \in F, \qquad (2.6)$$

so that the combinatory cost of the algorithm ϕ_ε is much smaller than the information complexity of the problem. Then

$$\text{comp}(\varepsilon) \approx \text{cost}(U_\varepsilon) \approx c\,m(\varepsilon),$$

and thus ϕ_ε is an almost optimal algorithm and N_ε is almost optimal information.

Remark: The assumption (2.6) holds for many problems. In particular, when $c \gg 1$, the relation (2.6) holds whenever there exists a linear optimal error algorithm, i.e., the minimal error among algorithms using that information is attained by a linear combination of the information values. For example, the modified trapezoid rule (2.2) is a linear optimal error algorithm for the integration problem. For further information, see the review article Packel [1988]. □

Remark: Although we have only used information complexity as a tool for determining problem complexity, there are other areas (such as computational learning theory) where information complexity is the key issue. See, e.g., Haussler [1988] for further discussion. □

Remark: We have seen that information-based techniques produce tight complexity bounds whenever the information complexity dominates the combinatory complexity. Of course, this won't always happen; the combinatory complexity may dominate the information complexity. One example (using the Turing machine model of computation) is provided by the problem of decentralized control discussed in Papadimitriou & Tsitsiklis [1986]. They found the information complexity to be $\Theta(\varepsilon^{-4})$. However, the combinatory complexity is polynomial in $1/\varepsilon$ iff P = NP. Hence it is very likely that the combinatory complexity greatly dominates the information complexity for this problem. An extreme example is given by Wasilkowski & Woźniakowski [1993], who produced a linear problem having finite information complexity, but with infinite combinatory complexity. □

2.3 An Example: Integration (Concluded)

Let us see how this all applies to the univariate integration problem mentioned at the beginning of this chapter. We once again emphasize that we have chosen the worst case setting. Here, the set

$$F = \{\, [0,1] \xrightarrow{f} \mathbb{R} : \mathrm{Lip}(f) \le L \,\}$$

of problem elements consists of all Lipschitz continuous functions whose Lipschitz constant is at most L, the set G of solution elements is $\mathbb{R}$, and the solution operator $S \colon F \to G$ is given by

$$S(f) = \int_0^1 f(x)\, dx \qquad \forall f \in F.$$

The only permissible information operations are function evaluations $f(x)$ for problem elements $f \in F$ and sample points $x \in [0,1]$. So information for our problem has the form

$$N(f) = [f(t_1), \ldots, f(t_n)], \qquad (2.7)$$

where the evaluation points $t_1, \ldots, t_n \in [0,1]$ determining the information N may be chosen either adaptively or nonadaptively. Note that since $G = \mathbb{R}$, the vector space operations permitted by our model of computation are merely real addition and multiplication.

From the analysis in Section 2.1, we see that no matter how the points $t_1, \ldots, t_n$ are chosen, the modified trapezoidal rule has minimal error among all algorithms using the information (2.7).† Furthermore, if the information N is nonadaptive, then zero data provides the worst case, and it is easy to see (see Figure 2.1) that

$$e^{\mathrm{wor}}(\phi^*, N) = r^{\mathrm{wor}}(N) = \sup_{\substack{h \in F \\ h(t_1) = \cdots = h(t_n) = 0}} \int_0^1 h(x)\, dx$$

$$= L \cdot \left(\tfrac{1}{2} t_1^2 + \tfrac{1}{4} \sum_{i=1}^{n-1} (t_{i+1} - t_i)^2 + \tfrac{1}{2} (1 - t_n)^2 \right). \qquad (2.8)$$

We now settle the question of adaption vs. nonadaption. Let N^{a} be adaptive information. We then let N^{non} be N^{a} for the zero function. That is, we first let $n = n(0)$, the number of sample points used when

---

† We emphasize that the modified trapezoidal rule is optimal only because we chose the integrand class to consist of functions with a given bound on the Lipschitz constant. If we had chosen a different class of integrands, such as the class of functions whose rth derivative was bounded, an entirely different approximation would be optimal, see, e.g., Traub *et al.* [1988], pp. 117–137.

the function f is the zero function, and we then choose sample points $t_1, \ldots, t_n$ for the information N^{non} as the same sample points that would be used for the zero function. Since the integral is a linear functional and the class of integrands is balanced (symmetric about the origin) and convex, we know that $r(N^{\text{non}}) \leq r(N^{\text{a}})$, see, e.g., pp. 57–65 of Traub *et al.* [1988]. That is, given adaptive information, we can find nonadaptive information of the same cardinality or less, having the same radius or less. This means that we can restrict ourselves to nonadaptive information. (See Kon & Novak [1990] and Novak [1996] for further discussion about adaption vs. nonadaption.)

Now let $N(f) = [f(t_1), \ldots, f(t_n)]$ be nonadaptive information. If we let $r^{\text{wor}}(n)$ denote the minimal value of $r^{\text{wor}}(N)$ over all information of cardinality n, a straightforward calculation using (2.8) yields that

$$r^{\text{wor}}(n) = \frac{L}{4n}, \tag{2.9}$$

and that the information

$$r^{\text{wor}}(N_n) = [f(t_1^*), \ldots, f(t_n^*)],$$

with sample points given by

$$t_i^* = \frac{2i - 1}{2n} \qquad (1 \leq i \leq n), \tag{2.10}$$

is nth optimal information, i.e., information of cardinality n having minimal radius. We then see that the modified trapezoidal rule using these sample points is an nth minimal error algorithm, i.e., its error is minimal among all algorithms using any information of cardinality at most n. Note that the modified trapezoidal rule using the optimal information N_n has the especially simple form

$$U_n(f) \equiv \phi^*(N_n(f)) := \frac{1}{n} \sum_{i=1}^{n} f(t_i^*), \tag{2.11}$$

which is the composite midpoint rule using equal subintervals. Clearly, we can calculate $U_n(f)$ with cost at most $(c + 1)n$.

From (2.9), we see that the ε-cardinality number for our problem is

$$m^{\text{wor}}(\varepsilon) = \left\lceil \frac{L}{4\varepsilon} \right\rceil.$$

Thus the ε-complexity of our integration problem satisfies

$$\text{comp}^{\text{wor}}(\varepsilon) \geq c \left\lceil \frac{L}{4\varepsilon} \right\rceil. \tag{2.12}$$

On the other hand, choosing $n = m(\varepsilon)$ and using the algorithm (2.11) with sample points given by (2.10), we see that the resulting approximation U_ε computes an ε-approximation, with

$$\text{cost}^{\text{wor}}(U_\varepsilon) \leq (c+1)\left\lceil \frac{L}{4\varepsilon} \right\rceil. \tag{2.13}$$

Comparing (2.12) and (2.13), we see that

$$c\left\lceil \frac{L}{4\varepsilon} \right\rceil \leq \text{comp}^{\text{wor}}(\varepsilon) \leq \text{cost}^{\text{wor}}(U_\varepsilon) \leq (c+1)\left\lceil \frac{L}{4\varepsilon} \right\rceil. \tag{2.14}$$

Note the extremely tight lower and upper bounds on the complexity.

Remark: Note that the complexity depends on L, the known bound on the Lipschitz constant. However, the nth minimal error algorithm (the midpoint rule with equal subintervals) is independent of L. This means that even if we don't know L, we do know how to get the smallest error for a given number of evaluations. As to the size of the error, we only know that

$$|S(f) - U_n(f)| \leq \frac{\text{Lip}(f)}{4n}.$$

□

Since we generally expect that $c \gg 1$, the bounds in (2.14) are very tight. (For example, if $c = 100$, i.e., function evaluation is 100 times as hard as an arithmetic operation, then the two bounds are within 1% of each other.) Hence the worst case ε-complexity of our problem is roughly $(cL)/(4\varepsilon)$, and U_ε is a nearly optimal approximation.

3

Breaking the Curse of Dimensionality

In the previous chapter, we introduced basic concepts, using univariate integration as a running example. However, most mathematical models are multivariate. For example:

- **Science:** Many problems involving multi-particle systems yield mathematical formulations of high dimension. For example, if we want to find the wave function of a uranium atom's electron cloud, we solve Schrödinger's equation in $3 \times 92 = 276$ dimensions.
- **Economics:** Markovian decision processes arise in economics and operation research; see, e.g., Bellman [1957]. Here, two parameters determine the dimension of the problem, namely d_s and d_c, which are the respective numbers of components in the state and control variables.
- **Finance:** Suppose that a financial institution wants to value a pool of 30-year mortgages, whose value depends on the proportion of borrowers who refinance their loans and on future interest rates. If we permit monthly refinancing, then this task can be expressed as the evaluation of integrals depending on $30 \times 12 = 360$ variables. See Fabozzi [1992] for further discussion of such collateralized mortgage obligations.

Often, multivariate problems suffer from the "curse of dimensionality," described below, if one insists on a guarantee of an error at most ε for every input (i.e., a worst case assurance). For such problems, there are only two possible ways to attempt to break the curse of dimensionality:

- We can weaken the worst case guarantee, accepting instead a stochastic assurance. As we shall see, for some problems, we can break the curse of dimensionality by weakening the assurance; for others, we cannot.

- We can change the class F of inputs. By suitable choices of F, we can sometimes provide a worst case guarantee while breaking intractability.

We shall explore both alternatives in this chapter.

We will focus on a multivariate numerical integration problem, which we shall denote by INT. We do this for a number of reasons.

(i) Many of the issues that arise in general occur for this problem.

(ii) Multivariate integration is ubiquitous, arising in numerous applications.

(iii) More IBC research has been done on the computational complexity of multivariate integration than on any other problem.

Write $D = [0,1]^d$ for the d-dimensional unit cube. Let F be a class of real-valued functions defined over D. Then our solution operator is

$$S(f) = \int_D f(x)\, dx \equiv \int_{[0,1]^d} f(x_1, \ldots, x_d)\, dx_1 \ldots dx_d. \qquad (3.1)$$

The class of permissible information operations will be function evaluations, i.e., we can evaluate $f(x)$ for any $x \in D$ and any $f \in F$.

Our integrand class is to have "smoothness r." One way of defining such a class is to let F consist of those functions whose derivatives of order through r satisfy a known a priori bound. We shall assume this bound to be 1 without essential loss of generality. More precisely, we let $F = F_r$ where

$$F_r := \{\, D \xrightarrow{f} \mathbb{R} : D^\alpha f \text{ is continuous for all } |\alpha| \leq r,$$
$$\|D^\alpha f\|_{\max} \leq 1 \text{ for all } |\alpha| \leq r \,\}.$$

Here

$$\|g\|_{\max} = \max_{x \in D} |g(x)|.$$

Moreover, we use the standard multi-index notations

$$D^\alpha = \left(\frac{\partial}{\partial x_1}\right)^{\alpha_1} \cdots \left(\frac{\partial}{\partial x_d}\right)^{\alpha_d}$$

and

$$|\alpha| = \alpha_1 + \cdots + \alpha_d,$$

with $\alpha = (\alpha_1, \ldots, \alpha_d)$ a vector of non-negative integers. In short, we are looking at functions having total smoothness r in the sense of the sup-norm.

Assume that $\varepsilon < 1$. Bakhvalov [1959] showed that the ε-complexity of the d-dimensional integration problem for integrands of total smoothness r is†

$$\text{comp}^{\text{wor}}(\varepsilon, d, \text{INT}) = \Theta \left(c(d) \left(\frac{1}{\varepsilon} \right)^{d/r} \right). \qquad (3.2)$$

Here, we write $c(d)$ for the cost of a function evaluation, reinforcing the idea that this may depend on d. Note that the right-hand side of (3.2) is multiplied by a factor that is independent of ε, but may depend on r and d.

Remark: There are several ways of defining a class of problem elements "having smoothness r." It might be simpler to choose $F = F_r^*$, where

$$F_r^* := \{\, D \xrightarrow{f} \mathbb{R} : D^\alpha f \text{ is continuous for all } |\alpha| \le r,$$
$$\|D^\alpha f\|_{\max} \le 1 \text{ for all } |\alpha| = r \,\},$$

i.e., we only ask that the rth derivatives be bounded by 1. However, it is often easier to derive results for the class F_r than for F_r^*.

What is the difference between these two classes? In the class F_r^*, we only control the size of the rth-order derivatives, whereas in the class F_r we control the size of *all* derivatives of order at most r. Another way of looking at the difference between the two classes is that F_r^* consists of all functions having a Sobolev *seminorm* bounded by 1, whereas F_r consists of all functions having a Sobolev *norm* bounded by 1. Thus although F_r may at first appear to be more complicated than F_r^*, the class F_r is merely the unit ball of a Sobolev space.

How are complexity results for the classes F_r and F_r^* related?

Suppose first that d and r are fixed. Note that an element of F_r^* may be represented as the sum of an element of F_r and a d-variate polynomial of degree at most $r - 1$. Hence complexity results for the classes will be asymptotically the same as $\varepsilon \to 0$ with fixed d and r.

Now suppose that d or r is allowed to vary. (We are especially interested in the case that d attains large values.) It is clear that $F_r \subset F_r^*$.

---

† We use the Θ-notation of Knuth [1976], writing $f = \Omega(g)$ iff $g = O(f)$, and $f = \Theta(g)$ iff $f = O(g)$ and $g = O(f)$. Some authors write $f \asymp g$ instead of $f = \Theta(g)$.

Hence any negative result (such as an exponential lower bound on complexity) on the class F_r also applies to the class F_r^*. □

What does (3.2) tell us?

First, suppose that $r = 0$, which means that the integrands are continuous, with a known bound. Then the exponent appearing in (3.2) is infinite, which means that the ε-complexity is infinite. If the ε-complexity is infinite, we say the problem is *unsolvable*.

Suppose now that $r > 0$. Then the ε-complexity is finite for any ε, d, and r. However, for fixed values of the smoothness r and the desired error ε, we find that the complexity depends exponentially on the dimension d. Bellman [1957] called exponential dependence on dimension "the curse of dimensionality." † This was based on experience, not theorems of computational complexity. Thus in the worst case setting, multivariate integration for the class F_r suffers from the curse of dimensionality.

To see why this exponential dependence of complexity on dimension is ominous, let us consider the case of a three-dimensional integral $(d = 3)$, the integrands having one derivative $(r = 1)$. Suppose for the sake of argument that we choose $\varepsilon = 10^{-6}$, i.e., we want six-place accuracy. Then (ignoring the Θ-constant) we need to compute 10^{18} function values. Let us further make the *highly* optimistic assumption that the evaluation of any integrand at any point requires only one *flop* (floating point operation). Then to calculate an ε-approximation, we need to perform 10^{18} flops. Now suppose that our computer can compute 10^{10} flops per second. It follows that we will need 10^8 seconds to calculate an ε-approximation, i.e., more than three years!

Now recall that in discrete computational complexity theory, we say that a problem is tractable iff the problem complexity grows at most polynomially with some parameter, such as the size of the input. (See, e.g., Garey & Johnson [1979] for further discussion.) Borrowing this concept, we will say that the tractability of a problem with respect to some parameter depends on whether the complexity has at most polynomial growth in that parameter. More precisely:

- A problem is *tractable in* $1/\varepsilon$ if there exist a function K and a number p such that $\mathrm{comp}(\varepsilon, d) \leq (c(d) + 2)K(d)(1/\varepsilon)^p$ for all d and all $\varepsilon \in (0, 1]$. For brevity, we shall often say that a problem is *tractable* if it is tractable in $1/\varepsilon$.

† Although we prefer the shorter phrase "the curse of dimension," we will stay with common usage and use Bellman's phrase.

- A problem is *tractable in d* if there exist a function K and a number p such that $\mathrm{comp}(\varepsilon, d) \le (c(d) + 2)K(\varepsilon)d^p$ for all d and all $\varepsilon \in (0,1]$.

(We use $c(d) + 2$ rather than $c(d)$ in these definitions merely as a technical convenience; see Woźniakowski [1994b] for further discussion.) The number p must be independent of d and ε. The best value of p is called the *exponent* of the problem; it need not be an integer. A problem that is not tractable in $1/\varepsilon$ or d is said to be *intractable* in $1/\varepsilon$ or d, respectively. If a problem is intractable in either $1/\varepsilon$ or d we shall say, for simplicity, that the problem is *intractable*.

Thus integration for F_r is intractable for the worst case setting.

Of course, one might hope that integration is merely a pathological problem, and that the complexity of other important multivariate problems will not depend exponentially on the dimension. However, there are many problems whose ε-complexity is of the form (3.2) when the class of problem elements is F_r. Examples include:

- approximation (see Novak [1988a] and Pinkus [1985]),
- partial differential equations (see Chapter 5 of Werschulz [1991]),
- integral equations (see Chapter 6 of Werschulz [1991]),
- Markovian decision processes (as described above, with $d = 2d_s + d_c$, see Chow & Tsitsiklis [1989], [1991]),
- nonlinear optimization (see Nemirovsky & Yudin [1983]).

Remark: An important difference between discrete complexity theory and information-based complexity is that the intractability of many discrete problems is only *conjectured*, while the intractability of many IBC problems has been *proven*. Intractability has been proven for many IBC problems because of arguments at the information level. This level typically does not exist in discrete complexity and therefore we have to settle for trying to establish a complexity hierarchy.   □

How can we hope to solve intractable problems? One idea that will *not* work will be to look for a more clever approximation, that is, a better choice of information and algorithm. This is because intractability results tell us that the complexity, i.e., minimal cost among *all* approximations, grows exponentially. Hence there is no approximation that can break the curse of dimensionality.

We use integration as an example of how we might break intractability. Since intractability is a consequence of our formulation, we consider the underlying assumptions:

(i) We are using the worst case setting.

(ii) The set of inputs is F_r.

If we are going to break intractability, we will have to change at least one of these assumptions.

We first look at relaxing restriction (i). In other words, we will change the setting. Note that when we do this, we make a tradeoff. We weaken the assurance granted by the worst case setting, hoping that we will break intractability.

The first alternative setting we'll consider is the *randomized* setting. In the worst case setting, we assumed that the information and algorithm were given deterministically. Here, we use *randomized information* of the form

$$N_\tau(f) = [f(t_1), \ldots, f(t_{n_\tau})]$$

where n_τ and each t_i depend on the parameter τ, which is chosen at random from some set T according to a probability measure ρ on T. (For example, we might set $n_\tau = n$, and choose components $t_{i,j}$ of the sample point $t_i = (t_{i,1}, \ldots, t_{i,d}) \in D$ as independent random variables according to the uniform distribution over the unit interval. In this case, $T = [0,1]^{nd}$ and ρ is the uniform distribution over T.) We allow adaption, i.e., each t_i may possibly depend on the samples calculated previously, and we also allow the total number $n_\tau = n_\tau(f)$ to be adaptively determined. The choice of algorithm ϕ_τ is also allowed to depend on the randomly chosen τ, i.e., we use *randomized algorithms* producing randomized approximations $U_\tau = \phi_\tau(N_\tau(f))$. We complete our definition of the randomized setting by setting

$$\mathrm{card}(N) = \mathrm{card}^{\mathrm{ran}}(N) := \sup_{f \in F} \int_T n_\tau(f)\, \rho(d\tau),$$

$$e(U) = e^{\mathrm{ran}}(U) := \left(\sup_{f \in F} \int_T |S(f) - U_\tau(f)|^2\, \rho(d\tau) \right)^{1/2},$$

$$\mathrm{cost}(U) = \mathrm{cost}^{\mathrm{ran}}(U) := \sup_{f \in F} \int_T \mathrm{cost}(U_\tau, f)\, \rho(d\tau).$$

In the randomized setting, we guarantee that $e^{\mathrm{ran}}(U)$ is at most ε. The complexity $\mathrm{comp}^{\mathrm{ran}}(\varepsilon)$ is the minimal cost of computing an ε-approximation in the randomized setting. Since any deterministic approximation can be treated as a randomized approximation (for a measure ρ concentrated on one element), it is clear that

$$\mathrm{comp}^{\mathrm{ran}}(\varepsilon) \le \mathrm{comp}^{\mathrm{wor}}(\varepsilon). \tag{3.3}$$

The hope is that we can do *much* better in the randomized setting than in the deterministic worst case setting.

Remark: For simplicity, we have only defined the randomized setting for the integration problem. The randomized setting can also be defined for problems in normed linear spaces, with the absolute value replaced by a norm. □

The Monte Carlo algorithm (Metropolis & Ulam [1949]) is the classical example of an algorithm using randomized information. See Heinrich [1996] for a survey of the complexity theory of Monte Carlo algorithms.

We again consider integration as our example. We choose sample values $t_1, \ldots, t_n$ independently from the uniform distribution ρ_{unif} on $[0,1]^d$. Then the Monte Carlo algorithm computes an approximation

$$S(f) = \int_{[0,1]^d} f(x)\, dx \approx U_\tau^{\mathrm{mc}}(f) := \frac{1}{n} \sum_{i=1}^n f(t_i).$$

We find that

$$\int_{[0,1]^{nd}} |S(f) - U_\tau^{\mathrm{mc}}(f)|^2 \, dt_1\, dt_2 \ldots dt_n = \frac{\mathrm{var}(f)}{n},$$

where

$$\mathrm{var}(f) = \int_D f(x)^2 \, dx - \left(\int_D f(x)\, dx \right)^2$$

is the variance of f. Suppose now that our set F of problem inputs is such that $\sup_{f \in F} \mathrm{var}(f) = 1$. (For instance, this holds when F is the unit ball of $C(D)$, the space of all continuous functions on D.) Then

$$e^{\mathrm{ran}}(U^{\mathrm{mc}}) = \frac{1}{\sqrt{n}}. \tag{3.4}$$

Hence $\lceil (1/\varepsilon)^2 \rceil$ function evaluations are necessary and sufficient for the Monte Carlo algorithm to compute an ε-approximation in the randomized setting. This is independent of the dimension d of the cube over which we are integrating. Hence the integration problem is tractable in $1/\varepsilon$ for the randomized setting, with exponent at most 2.

Remark: Suppose that F is the unit ball of $C(D)$. Then $\mathrm{comp}^{\mathrm{ran}}(\varepsilon) = \Theta(\varepsilon^{-2})$ (see Bakhvalov [1959], Novak [1988b]) and so the Monte Carlo algorithm is optimal (to within a constant factor). Mathé [1995] has determined that the nth *minimal radius* (i.e., the minimal error achieved by algorithms using at most n function evaluations) for this class F is

$$\frac{1}{1 + \sqrt{n},}$$

and that this error is attained by

$$\frac{1}{n + \sqrt{n}} \sum_{i=1}^{n} f(t_i),$$

a modification of the classical Monte Carlo algorithm. It then follows that $\text{comp}^{\text{ran}}(\varepsilon) = c(d)\varepsilon^{-2}(1 + o(1))$. $\qquad\qquad\square$

Thus randomization breaks intractability for the integration problem. Why should picking sample points at random be much better than picking them deterministically in the optimal way? This is possible because we have replaced the absolute assurance of the worst case setting by the stochastic assurance of the randomized setting. *There's no free lunch!*

Remark: Of course, the usual implementation of the Monte Carlo algorithm does not use random numbers. Typically, a pseudorandom number generator, such as a linear congruential generator (LCG), is used. Traub & Woźniakowski [1992] studied the Monte Carlo algorithm using pseudorandom numbers. They found both bad news and good news. The bad news is that if the generator is capable of producing only finitely many points, then pseudorandom Monte Carlo fails for functions in the unit ball of $C(D)$, even though Monte Carlo has theoretical cost $\Theta(c(d)(1/\varepsilon^2))$ for calculating an ε-approximation over this class.

What happens when a smaller class of integrands is used? In particular, consider the class of Lipschitz functions, where the Lipschitz constant has a known uniform bound L. Traub & Woźniakowski [1992] obtained worst case results for this class, assuming (without loss of generality) that $L = 1$. They prove a lower bound of roughly $(k^*)^{-1/d}$ for the Monte Carlo algorithm with an arbitrary pseudorandom number generator, where k^* is the total number of points that the pseudorandom generator is capable of producing. In particular, if an LCG is used with only one initial seed, then pseudorandom Monte Carlo fails. In particular, if the dimension d is 10 and the LCG can produce 2^{30} points, the error of the pseudorandom Monte Carlo method is at least $\frac{5}{58}$. On the other hand, suppose that a linear congruential generator of period at least $\sqrt{n}$ is used for each component, with independent uniformly distributed initial seeds. Then the good news is that pseudorandom Monte Carlo using n function values has expected error roughly $n^{-1/2}$ over the class, i.e., pseudorandom Monte Carlo behaves roughly the same as the Monte Carlo method with random points, provided the functions are somewhat smoother and suitable precautions are taken with the pseudorandom number generator.   □

The cost of Monte Carlo is *always* $\Theta(c(d)(1/\varepsilon^2))$, independent of the smoothness of the integrand class. That is, the Monte Carlo algorithm does not take advantage of the smoothness of the class of integrands. Suppose that we are using the class F_r, so that our problem elements have smoothness r. There is a method due to Bakhvalov [1959] using randomized information that does take advantage of the smoothness, and whose error (when n evaluations are used) is $\Theta(1/n^\sigma)$, where

$$\sigma = \frac{2d}{2r + d}.$$

Moreover, Bakhvalov proved that the nth minimal error is $\Theta(1/n^\sigma)$ if n_τ is constant; this result was extended to the case of varying n_τ by Novak [1988b]. Hence, Bakhvalov's algorithm is optimal, and

$$\text{comp}^{\text{ran}}(\varepsilon, d, \text{INT}) = \Theta\left(c(d)\left(\frac{1}{\varepsilon}\right)^\sigma\right). \tag{3.5}$$

Special cases of Bakhvalov's result are often rediscovered. People have repeatedly told us that they have discovered an improvement of the Monte Carlo method, with faster convergence. This is only possible if they are assuming more smoothness than that required by Monte Carlo.

What can we infer from this result? First, suppose that $r = 0$. We then see that the ε-complexity in the randomized setting is $\Theta(\varepsilon^{-2})$. This implies that the Monte Carlo algorithm is optimal when $r = 0$. However, when $r > 0$, we find $\sigma < 2$, and so the Monte Carlo algorithm is no longer optimal. However, the margin of non-optimality gets smaller as d increases for fixed r.

So randomization breaks intractability for the integration problem over F_r. Unfortunately there are intractable problems for which randomization doesn't help:

Example: Consider APP, a *(function) approximation problem*. Here, we let our solution operator $S\colon F_r \to C(D)$ be the embedding of F_r into the space $C(D)$ of continuous functions under the sup norm, so that $S(f) = f$ for all $f \in F_r$. Once again, we let function evaluations be our permissible information operations. Then

$$\text{comp}^{\text{wor}}(\varepsilon, d, \text{APP}) = \Theta\left(c(d)\left(\frac{1}{\varepsilon}\right)^{d/r}\right)$$

(see, e.g., the discussion in Novak [1988a]). Hence in the worst case setting, the approximation problem is intractable in $1/\varepsilon$. Since randomization breaks intractability for integration, we might hope that the same holds for approximation. Unfortunately, we find that

$$\text{comp}^{\text{ran}}(\varepsilon, d, \text{APP}) = \Theta\left(c(d)\left(\frac{1}{\varepsilon}\right)^{d/r}\right),$$

see Wasilkowski [1989c]. Hence randomization does not break intractability. □

There are many other problems for which randomization doesn't break intractability. Important examples include the solution of elliptic partial differential equations and of Fredholm integral equations of the second kind, see Chapter 8, Section 3 in Werschulz [1991]. It is natural to pose the following

---

Open Problem: Characterize the problems for which randomization breaks intractability.

There is another setting that we can use to try to break the worst case intractability of the integration problem. Suppose that we have a probability measure μ on the class F of problem elements. Then the *average case setting* is defined by choosing

$$\text{card}(N) \equiv \text{card}^{\text{avg}}(N) := \int_F n(f)\,\mu(df),$$

$$e(U) \equiv e^{\text{avg}}(U) := \left(\int_F |S(f) - U(f)|^2\,\mu(df)\right)^{1/2},$$

$$\text{cost}(U) \equiv \text{cost}^{\text{avg}}(U) := \int_F \text{cost}(U, f)\,\mu(df).$$

In the average case setting, we provide the assurance that the expected error is at most ε. The complexity, comp^{avg}, is the minimal expected cost. Clearly

$$\text{comp}^{\text{avg}}(\varepsilon) \leq \text{comp}^{\text{wor}}(\varepsilon). \tag{3.6}$$

Once again, we hope that we might succeed in breaking intractability in this setting.

Remark: For simplicity, we have only defined the average case setting for the integration problem. The average case setting can also be defined for problems in normed linear spaces, with the absolute value replaced by a norm.   □

We briefly contrast the randomized and average case settings. In the randomized setting, we allow nondeterminism in our choice of information and algorithm; we then settle for a worst case expected error over all problem elements, the expectation being with respect to the distribution generating the information and the algorithm. In the average case setting, the information and algorithm are chosen deterministically; we then settle for an expected error with respect to a measure on the problem elements.

In what follows, we will generally assume (unless stated otherwise) that one of the following holds:

(i) F is a separable Banach space, and μ is a zero mean *Gaussian* measure, which means that the values of any bounded linear functional on F are normally distributed with zero mean. (See Kuo [1975], Skorohod [1974], Vakhania *et al.* [1987], and Appendix 2 in Traub *et al.* [1988] for more information on Gaussian measures.)

(ii) F is a ball of finite radius in a separable Banach space, and μ is a truncated Gaussian measure on F.

Provided that the radius of the ball in (ii) is sufficiently large, the average case complexity using the truncated Gaussian measure over a ball is essentially the same as the complexity using the Gaussian measure over the whole space; see pp. 257–268 of Traub *et al.* [1988]. Therefore in what follows, we will not distinguish between average case complexity results for these two possibilities.

Remark: Note the difference between the worst case and randomized settings on the one hand, and the average case setting on the other. For many problems, the worst case or randomized complexity over the whole space is infinite, whereas the complexity over a ball is finite. However, the average case complexities for problems over either a sufficiently large ball or the whole space are comparable.   □

Modulo multiplicative constants of order one,

$$\mathrm{comp}^{\mathrm{avg}}(\varepsilon) \leq \mathrm{comp}^{\mathrm{ran}}(\varepsilon) \tag{3.7}$$

(see Section 11.3 of Traub *et al.* [1988]). Combining this with (3.3), we find that

$$\text{comp}^{\text{avg}}(\varepsilon) \leq \text{comp}^{\text{ran}}(\varepsilon) \leq \text{comp}^{\text{wor}}(\varepsilon). \tag{3.8}$$

Of course, since $\text{comp}^{\text{wor}}(\varepsilon)$ is typically exponential in d, we're only interested in dramatic improvements.

What is the average complexity of our integration problem? From (3.5) and (3.7), we know that integration is tractable on the average and that the average complexity is at most of order $1/\varepsilon^2$. However, this is only an existence proof, i.e., we know that there exist good sample points, for which an ε-approximation can be calculated at cost proportional to $1/\varepsilon^2$. We also want to know how to obtain these good points. The problem of selecting sample points to achieve good average cost has been open since Sacks & Ylvisaker [1966].

Assume that $r = 0$, that is, the integrands are continuous. Furthermore, assume that the measure on the space of integrands is the *Wiener sheet measure*, the Gaussian measure w whose mean is zero and that satisfies

$$\int_{C([0,1]^d)} f(x) f(t) \, w(df) = \prod_{i=1}^{d} \min\{x_i, t_i\},$$

see Adler [1981]. This measure, which arises in the study of Brownian motion, is one of the best-known Gaussian measures.

Regularly spaced grids are widely used in practice, for modest values of d. Are regular grids good on the average? We know the answer is "no," since the average cost of obtaining an ε-approximation is exponential in d if grid points are used, see Papageorgiou & Wasilkowski [1990].

Woźniakowski [1991] established the average complexity of this problem and found the optimal information and algorithm, by exploiting a relation between this problem and discrepancy theory, a much-studied branch of number theory. He showed that

$$\text{comp}^{\text{avg}}(\varepsilon, d, \text{INT}) = \Theta\left(c(d)\frac{1}{\varepsilon}\left(\log\frac{1}{\varepsilon}\right)^{(d-1)/2}\right). \tag{3.9}$$

Moreover, suppose we choose $t_i^* = \mathbf{1} - z_i^*$ for $1 \leq i \leq n$, where $\mathbf{1} = (1, \dots, 1)$ and the $z_1^*, \dots, z_n^*$ are shifted *Hammersley points*, see Hammersley [1960]. Then the algorithm

$$U(f) = \frac{1}{n}\sum_{i=1}^{n} f(t_i^*), \tag{3.10}$$

with

$$n = \Theta\left(\frac{1}{\varepsilon}\left(\log\frac{1}{\varepsilon}\right)^{(d-1)/2}\right),$$

is optimal (to within a constant factor, independent of ε). The proof of this result exploits work on L_2 discrepancy theory (Roth [1954], [1980]), as well as results in Wasilkowski [1986]. We note that Woźniakowski's algorithm is not fully constructive, since we do not know the amount by which we should shift the value of Hammersley points.

We defer further discussion of the implications of Woźniakowski's theorem, and the theory and applications of discrepancy theory, to Chapter 4.

Remark: What other multivariate problems are tractable on the average? Woźniakowski ([1992a], [1992b]) investigated the average complexity of linear multivariate problems, assuming that arbitrary continuous linear functionals are permissible information operations. He gave a simple condition that is necessary and sufficient for a linear multivariate problem (with solution operator S) to be tractable on the average, namely, that the sum of the n largest eigenvalues of the covariance operator of μS^{-1} must decrease at least as fast as a polynomial in n^{-1}. In particular, he showed that the average complexity of the approximation problem with $r = 0$ and with the Wiener sheet measure is given by

$$\mathrm{comp}^{\mathrm{avg}}(\varepsilon, d, \mathrm{APP}) = \Theta\left(c(d)\left(\frac{1}{\varepsilon}\right)^2\left(\log\frac{1}{\varepsilon}\right)^{d-1}\right).$$

Sampling at *hyperbolic-cross points*† (which are due to Babenko [1960] and Smolyak [1963], but are frequently rediscovered) is essentially optimal. Thus approximating continuous functions in the average case setting is tractable in $1/\varepsilon$.   □

Remark: Of course, the average case complexity depends on the measure. To drive this point home, consider what happens if we use the isotropic Wiener measure (also known as Brownian motion in Levy's sense) instead of the Wiener sheet measure. Wasilkowski [1993] studied integration and approximation in the average case setting for this measure, the problem elements once again consisting of continuous functions

---

† Hyperbolic-cross point methods are also known as "Boolean interpolation," "discrete blending," and "sparse grid" methods in the Western literature; see Novak & Ritter [1996c] for discussion and further references.

$(r = 0)$. He showed that

$$\text{comp}^{\text{avg}}(\varepsilon, d, \text{INT}) = \Theta\left(c(d)\left(\frac{1}{\varepsilon}\right)^{\frac{2}{1+1/d}}\right).$$

Optimal sample points are given in Ritter [1996b]. Note that the exponent of $1/\varepsilon$ is at most 2, so the integration problem is tractable for the isotropic Wiener measure.

Wasilkowski [1993] also studied approximation. He showed that

$$\text{comp}^{\text{avg}}(\varepsilon, d, \text{APP}) = \Theta\left(c(d)\left(\frac{1}{\varepsilon}\right)^{2d}\right)$$

for the isotropic Wiener measure, with regular grid points being almost optimal. This means that approximation is intractable in the average case setting using the isotropic Wiener measure. Thus, the average case setting is not a panacea for curing intractability. □

We now look at the second way of trying to break intractability, namely, choosing a different set of inputs. (See also p. 51, where changing the class of inputs might provide an explanation of why quasi-Monte Carlo methods are so effective for certain problems of mathematical finance.) We will look at a different notion for "integrands of smoothness r." Rather than use F_r, the class of all functions f such that $D^\alpha f$ is bounded for all $|\alpha| \leq r$, we use the unit ball $\widetilde{F}_r$ in the space of functions having *bounded mixed derivatives* This space contains functions whose smoothness in any particular direction is r. (See, e.g., Temlyakov [1989] for a precise definition.) In a certain sense, the smoothness of functions belonging to $\widetilde{F}_r$ increases if d increases even though r is held fixed; hence, it is plausible that integration might be tractable for $\widetilde{F}_r$.

First, we look at the complexity of integration in the *worst* case setting for the class $\widetilde{F}_r$. Using the results of Bykovskij [1985] and of Temlyakov [1990], it follows that

$$\text{comp}^{\text{wor}}(\varepsilon, d, \text{INT}) = \Theta\left(c(d)\left(\frac{1}{\varepsilon}\right)^{\frac{1}{r}}\left(\log\frac{1}{\varepsilon}\right)^{\frac{d-1}{2r}}\right).$$

What can we infer from this? If $r = 0$, the problem is unsolvable. However, the problem is tractable in $1/\varepsilon$ if $r > 0$.

Next, we consider the average case complexity. Our measure is the Wiener sheet measure on the space of functions having bounded mixed derivative of order up through r, or it can be the corresponding truncated measure on $\widetilde{F}_r$. Of course, since we know that integration is tractable in the average case setting for $r = 0$, it is certainly tractable for the case of $r \geq 0$; however, one would hope that one could do even better by taking advantage of the additional smoothness. Now there is an important relation between the worst and average case settings for the integration problem stating that the average case setting (with respect to a measure μ with covariance kernel R_μ) of the integration problem is equivalent to the worst case setting over the unit ball of the Hilbert space whose reproducing kernel is R_μ (see, e.g., Micchelli & Wahba [1981]). Exploiting this relation, Paskov [1993] proved that

$$\text{comp}^{\text{avg}}(\varepsilon, d, \text{INT}) = \Theta \left(c(d) \left(\frac{1}{\varepsilon} \right)^{\frac{1}{r+1}} \left(\log \frac{1}{\varepsilon} \right)^{\frac{d-1}{2(r+1)}} \right).$$

Basically, this states that the average case setting adds one derivative of smoothness, in each direction, to the worst case setting. In both the worst and average case settings, hyperbolic-cross points are almost optimal sample points, modulo a logarithmic factor.

Remark: We have seen that integration is tractable (even in the worst case setting) when we use spaces of bounded mixed derivatives. What happens when we use these spaces when solving the approximation problem? We first look at the worst case setting, which was studied in Temlyakov [1993]. Since the problem is unsolvable when $r = 0$, he restricted his study to the case $r \geq 1$. He found that

$$\text{comp}^{\text{wor}}(\varepsilon, d, \text{APP}) = \Theta \left(c(d) \left(\frac{1}{\varepsilon} \right)^{\frac{1}{r-1/2}} \left(\log \frac{1}{\varepsilon} \right)^{\frac{(d-1)r}{r-1/2}} \right),$$

with hyperbolic-cross points being almost optimal. The nearly optimal algorithm is based on the one developed in Temlyakov [1987], with an error estimate found in Temlyakov [1993]. The average case setting, with $r \geq 0$, was studied by Woźniakowski [1992b], who showed that

$$\text{comp}^{\text{avg}}(\varepsilon, d, \text{APP}) = \Theta \left(c(d) \left(\frac{1}{\varepsilon} \right)^{\frac{1}{r+1/2}} \left(\log \frac{1}{\varepsilon} \right)^{\frac{(d-1)(r+1)}{r+1/2}} \right),$$

with hyperbolic-cross points once again being almost optimal. $\square$

We end this chapter by reporting some recent results on *strong tractability*. So far, the formulas of this chapter have used Θ-notation, which shows dependence on $1/\varepsilon$ but hides factors that depend on d (and perhaps on r). For the high-dimensional problems that occur in many applications, these factors are crucial.

Estimates of these factors are currently not available, and obtaining them is believed to be very difficult. Klaus Roth, a 1958 Fields medalist, was unable to get estimates for the related problem of low discrepancy sequences. In 1992, Harald Niederreiter said (in a private communication to JFT) that he did not expect to see a good estimate in his lifetime.

Woźniakowski [1994b] finessed the problem of estimating these factors, by introducing a new concept. He said that a problem is *strongly tractable* if there exist non-negative numbers K and p such that

$$\text{comp}(\varepsilon, d) \leq (c(d) + 2) K \left(\frac{1}{\varepsilon}\right)^p \qquad (3.11)$$

for all positive integers d and all $\varepsilon \in (0, 1]$. The minimal p is called the *strong exponent* of the problem. He gave necessary and sufficient conditions for the tractability of linear problems in the worst and average case settings.

It might seem that strong tractability is too much to expect. Surprisingly, for some important cases, integration and approximation are both strongly tractable on the average! Wasilkowski & Woźniakowski [1995] established this by studying the strong tractability of multidimensional problems that are tensor products of one-dimensional problems. For example, multidimensional integration and approximation on the unit cube are tensor products of the corresponding one-dimensional problems on the unit interval. They showed that the strong tractability of the tensor product problem depends on the corresponding one-dimensional problem. The tensor product problem is strongly tractable whenever

- the corresponding one-dimensional problem has norm less than one, and
- there exists an algorithm that calculates an ε-approximation for the one-dimensional problem with cost polynomial in $1/\varepsilon$.

They also discussed the extent to which these two conditions are necessary. Furthermore, they constructed a *strongly polynomial time* algorithm, i.e., one that computes an ε-approximation with cost given by the right-hand side of (3.11). Their algorithm is based on Smolyak's algorithm (Smolyak [1963]), which is a tensor product of differences of one-dimensional algorithms. More recent work on tensor product problems may be found in Novak *et al.* [1997].

We provide an

Example (Integration): Consider the average case setting for continuous functions. Our measure is the Wiener sheet measure w on the space $C([0,1]^d)$ of continuous functions over $[0,1]^d$. One may check that

$$\int_{C([0,1]^d)} \left(\int_{[0,1]^d} f(x)\, dx \right)^2 w(df) = 3^{-d}.$$

Hence, for $\varepsilon \geq 3^{-d/2}$, the zero algorithm computes an ε-approximation at zero cost. For $\varepsilon < 3^{-d/2}$, we use Smolyak's algorithm, built up from the one-dimensional algorithm

$$U_m(f) = \frac{2}{2m+1} \sum_{i=1}^{m} f\left(\frac{2i}{2m+1} \right).$$

This algorithm computes an ε-approximation with cost at most

$$3.304(c(d)+2)\left(1.77959 + 2.714\frac{-1.12167 + \ln\varepsilon^{-1}}{d-1} \right)^{1.5(d-1)} \frac{1}{\varepsilon}. \quad (3.12)$$

Now the complexity of this problem is $\Theta(\varepsilon^{-1}(\ln\varepsilon^{-1})^{(d-1)/2})$. So the exponent of $1/\varepsilon$ agrees with the power of $1/\varepsilon$ in the complexity; however, the power of $\ln\varepsilon^{-1}$ is too big. Equation (3.12) yields an upper bound of

$$7.26(c(d)+2)\left(\frac{1}{\varepsilon} \right)^{2.454};$$

the details may be found in Wasilkowski & Woźniakowski [1995].

More recently, Wasilkowski & Woźniakowski [1997] have shown that the exponent can be reduced to 1.478. However, the proof of this latter result is *not* constructive.

Hence integration is strongly tractable in the average case setting for the Wiener sheet measure, with strong exponent at most 1.478. ☐

We close by posing the following

Open Problems: For a given strongly tractable problem,
▷ What are the best values for the exponent p and the constant K in (3.11)?
▷ Where are the best sample points for calculating an ε-approximation in d dimensions?

Part Two

Some Interesting Topics

4

Very High-Dimensional Integration and Mathematical Finance

The valuation of financial instruments often requires the calculation of very high-dimensional integrals. Dimensions of 360 and higher are not unusual. What do the complexity results of Chapter 3 suggest about the numerical calculation of such integrals? We recall several results of that chapter, for the convenience of the reader.

In the worst case setting for integrands of total smoothness r, the complexity of guaranteeing an answer to within ε is of order $(1/\varepsilon)^{d/r}$, where d is the dimension of the domain of integration. Hence if $r > 0$, the problem is intractable in dimension; if $r = 0$, it is unsolvable. To make the problem computationally feasible, we must either weaken the worst case assurance or change the class of inputs.

First, we describe replacing the worst case guarantee by a stochastic assurance. In the randomized setting, we settle for the expected cost of an approximation to be at most ε, where the expectation is with respect to the distribution determining the approximation. Suppose that we use information consisting of sample points chosen as independent uniformly distributed random variables from $[0,1]^d$. If $r = 0$, the Monte Carlo algorithm is optimal, and its complexity is of order $1/\varepsilon^2$. If $r > 0$, the complexity is of order $1/\varepsilon^\sigma$, where $\sigma < 2$. Hence in the randomized setting, integration is strongly tractable. Because of its $1/\varepsilon^2$ cost, Monte Carlo is widely used in many applications.

Can we do better than $1/\varepsilon^2$? The answer is "yes" if we're willing to shift to the average case setting. In this setting, we guarantee that the expected error is at most ε, where the expectation is now with respect to the measure on the space of integrands. Since the average case setting is *deterministic*, we would like a procedure for obtaining the sample points. The experimental design problem of selecting sample points with good average cost has been open since Sacks & Ylvisaker [1966].

It was settled by Woźniakowski [1991], for the case of the Wiener sheet measure on the space of continuous functions on $[0,1]^d$. Woźniakowski showed that the integrand should be evaluated at points that are related to low discrepancy points. Since discrepancy theory has been extensively studied in number theory, one could now draw on a very large existing literature.

Rather than attempting to select points from a uniform distribution, why not simply select uniform points deterministically? Uniformity is *not* sufficient, as the example of regular grids shows. Papageorgiou & Wasilkowski [1990] showed that the cost of any quadrature rule that used regular grid points is exponential in d.

What we desire is a "small" set of points in d dimensions, which is uniform. By *uniform*, we mean that the fraction of points lying within any rectangular subregion (with sides parallel to the coordinate axes) of the d-dimensional unit cube is as close as possible to the volume of that subregion. The *discrepancy* of a sequence of points is a measure of its deviation from uniformity; we therefore desire *low discrepancy*. The discrepancy can be measured in various ways; we confine ourselves here to L_2 and L_∞ discrepancy.

For $x = [x_1, \ldots, x_d] \in [0,1]^d$, define $[0,x) = [0,x_1) \times \cdots \times [0,x_d)$. Let $\chi_{[0,x)}$ be the characteristic function of $[0,x)$. For $t_1, \ldots, t_n \in [0,1]^d$, define

$$R_n(x, t_1, \ldots, t_n) = \frac{1}{n} \sum_{i=1}^{n} \chi_{[0,x)}(t_i) - \prod_{i=1}^{n} t_i.$$

The L_2 and L_∞ *discrepancy* are respectively defined as

$$D_{n,d}^{(2)}(t_1, \ldots, t_n) \equiv D_{n,d}^{(2)} = \left(\int_{[0,1]^d} R_n(x, t_1, \ldots, t_n)^2 \, dx \right)^{1/2}$$

and

$$D_{n,d}^{(\infty)}(t_1, \ldots, t_n) \equiv D_{n,d}^{(\infty)} = \sup_{x \in [0,1]^d} |R_n(x, t_1, \ldots, t_n)|.$$

For historical reasons, $D_{n,d}^{(\infty)}$ is usually written $D_{n,d}^*$, and we'll follow that usage here. See the monographs by Niederreiter [1992] and Drmota & Tichy [1997] for extensive material on discrepancy.

We next relate the average case L_2 integration error to the L_2 discrepancy. Let

$$I(f) = \int_{[0,1]^d} f(x) \, dx,$$

and let

$$U(f) = \frac{1}{n} \sum_{i=1}^{n} f(t_i),$$

for arbitrary $t_1, \ldots, t_n$. Let w be the classical Wiener sheet measure w on the space $C([0,1]^d)$ of continuous functions on $[0,1]^d$. Woźniakowski [1991] proved that the L_2 integration error is given by

$$\left(\int_{C([0,1]^d)} [I(f) - U(f)]^2 \, w(df) \right)^{1/2} = D_{n,d}^{(2)}(z_1, \ldots, z_n),$$

where

$$z_i = 1 - t_i \qquad \text{for } 1 \leq i \leq n. \tag{4.1}$$

Hence to minimize the average case L_2 integration error, we choose the sequence $t_1, \ldots, t_n \in [0,1]^d$ such that $D_{n,d}^{(2)}(z_1, \ldots, z_n)$ is as small as possible. Roth ([1954], [1980]) proved that

$$\inf_{z_1, \ldots, z_n \in [0,1]^d} D_{n,d}^{(2)}(z_1, \ldots, z_n) = \Theta\left(n^{-1}(\log n)^{(d-1)/2}\right). \tag{4.2}$$

Furthermore, the optimal z_i are related to Hammersley points.

We turn to the L_∞ discrepancy $D_{n,d}^*$. For our present purposes, the most important property of $D_{n,d}^*$ is given by the celebrated Koksma-Hlawka inequality (Niederreiter [1992], p. 20): if f has bounded variation $V(f)$ on $[0,1]^d$ (in the sense of Hardy and Krause), then for any points $t_1, \ldots, t_n \in [0,1]^d$, we have

$$|I(f) - U(f)| \leq V(f) D_{n,d}^*(t_1, \ldots, t_n). \tag{4.3}$$

We remark that $V(f)$ is finite if f has one derivative in each coordinate direction; however, the calculation of $V(f)$ for large d may be an onerous task, as its definition contains $2^d - 1$ terms.

To minimize the upper bound on the integration error in (4.3), we want to choose $t_1, \ldots, t_n$ so that $D_{n,d}^*(t_1, \ldots, t_n)$ is as small as possible. How small can that be? It is believed that

$$D_{n,d}^*(t_1, \ldots, t_n) \geq B_d \, n^{-1}(\log n)^{d-1} \qquad \forall \, n \geq 2,$$

where B_d depends only on the dimension d. Furthermore, there exist points $t_1^*, \ldots, t_n^* \in [0,1]^d$ such that

$$D_{n,d}^*(t_1^*, \ldots, t_n^*) = O\left(n^{-1}(\log n)^{d-1}\right).$$

More generally, any sequence $t_1, \ldots, t_n$ satisfying

$$D_{n,d}^*(t_1, \ldots, t_n) = O\left(n^{-1}(\log n)^d\right)$$

is said to be a *low discrepancy sequence* (LDS); see Niederreiter [1992] and Tezuka [1995]. Many examples of LDS are known, including Halton, Sobol', Hammersley, Faure, generalized Faure, and generalized Niederreiter sequences. Although many LDS share the same asymptotic behavior, their observed performance on important practical problems can differ widely, as we shall see below.

We compare and contrast the Woźniakowski and Koksma-Hlawka theorems. Woźniakowski's theorem states that to get optimal integration error averaged over a space of integrands, one should use points having minimal L_2 discrepancy. The Koksma-Hlawka theorem states that to minimize the upper bound on the integration error for any integrand of bounded variation, one should use points having minimal L_∞ discrepancy; that is, an LDS.

The motivation for looking at average behavior was to see if the Monte Carlo algorithm could be beaten. Recall that the expected error of the Monte Carlo algorithm is proportional to $n^{-1/2}$, while we've seen that there are deterministic sequences whose expected or worst case error is proportional to n^{-1} times a polylog factor. To fix ideas, let's focus on comparing $n^{-1/2}$ with $n^{-1}(\log n)^d$. What can we conclude?

- $n^{-1}(\log n)^d$ is asymptotically (in n) smaller than $n^{-1/2}$. This is why low discrepancy methods have long been of interest.
- For applications such as mathematical finance, n is modest in size while d is in the hundreds or thousands. Therefore, the asymptotic implications don't apply.

For d large and n fixed, the factor $(\log n)^d$ looks ominous. Therefore, leading experts believed that LDS should not be used for high-dimensional problems. For example, $d = 12$ was considered high by Bratley *et al.* [1992].

We'll estimate $\int_{[0,1]^d} f(x)\, dx$ by $n^{-1} \sum_{i=1}^n f(t_i)$. If the t_i are chosen at random, this is the Monte Carlo (MC) algorithm. If the t_i are chosen from a (deterministic) LDS, this is a quasi-Monte Carlo (QMC) algorithm. We believe that the term "quasi-Monte Carlo algorithm" is somewhat misleading because these algorithms are completely deterministic; however, since this term is so widely used, we will follow the general usage.

In 1992, one of us (JFT) and a then Ph.D. student (S. Paskov) followed a suggestion of I. Vanderhoof to test the efficacy of QMC algorithms for the valuation of financial derivatives. A *financial derivative* is a financial instrument whose value is derived from an underlying asset. At the time of this writing (1998) it is estimated that there are some ten to twenty trillion dollars in assets covered by financial derivatives. The valuation of financial derivatives is therefore of considerable interest to the financial community and a fascinating problem for the computational scientist.

The valuation of financial derivatives often requires very high-dimensional integration. Boyle [1977] suggested the use of MC, which became a major computational tool in the financial community.

The model problem chosen to compare the efficacy of QMC with MC was a 30-year Collateralized Mortgage Obligation (CMO). The particular CMO chosen required the computation of ten 360-dimensional integrals (360 being the number of months in thirty years). Since the model problem required some 10^5 floating point operations per sample point, it was important to use as few points as possible. See Paskov [1997] for a description of the CMO.

Software construction and testing of QMC methods for financial computations were begun in Fall, 1992. The first published announcement about the empirical results was in Traub & Woźniakowski [1994]. Details were reported in Paskov & Traub [1995], Papageorgiou & Traub [1996], and Paskov [1997]. For a popular account, see Cipra [1996].

We mention here a few of the empirical results from Paskov & Traub [1995]. Two QMC algorithms based on Halton and Sobol' points were compared with the Monte Carlo algorithm.

- Both QMC algorithms outperformed the MC algorithm.
- The convergence of the QMC algorithms was much smoother than that of the MC algorithm. This makes automatic termination of QMC easier and more reliable than MC.
- MC is very sensitive to the initial seed.

We next summarize empirical results of Papageorgiou & Traub [1996]. They compared QMC using the generalized Faure sequence (see Tezuka [1995]) and using a modified Sobol' sequence. It must be stressed that the results reported below are for the *modified* Sobol' sequence. Published Sobol' sequences (such as in Press *et al.* [1992]) will not lead to such results. We refer to the two QMC algorithms as QMC-GF and QMC-MS, respectively.

The conclusions regarding the valuation of the CMO model problem can be divided into three groups. Similar results hold for other derivatives, such as Asian options.

(i) QMC and MC Algorithms

Both QMC *algorithms beat the* MC *algorithm by a wide margin.*
In particular:

- Both the QMC-GF and the QMC-MS algorithms converge significantly faster than the MC algorithm.
- The QMC-GF algorithm always converges at least as fast as the QMC-MS algorithm, and frequently faster.
- The MC algorithm is sensitive to the initial seed.

(ii) Small Number of Sample Points

QMC *algorithms outperform the* MC *algorithm for a small number of sample points.*
In particular:

- QMC algorithms attain small error with a small number of points.
- For the hardest of the ten integrals required for the CMO valuation, the QMC-GF algorithm achieves accuracy 10^{-2} with just 170 points, while QMC-MS uses 600 points. On the other hand, the MC algorithm requires 2700 points for the same accuracy.
- The MC algorithm tends to waste points due to clustering, which severely compromises its performance when the sample size is small.

(iii) Speedup

The advantage of QMC *algorithms over the* MC *algorithm is further amplified as the accuracy demands grow.*
In particular:

- QMC algorithms are 20 to 50 times faster than the MC algorithm with even moderate sample sizes (2000 deterministic points or more).
- When high accuracy is desired, QMC algorithms can be 1000 times faster than MC.

We amplify a number of these points. The fact that the QMC-GF algorithm achieves accuracy 10^{-2} with just 170 points is particularly important for financial computations. Since the interest and prepayment functions have considerable uncertainty, people in the financial community find valuations whose accuracy is one part in a hundred to be sufficient. Furthermore, very rapid valuations are important because a financial institution may have a large book of instruments which have to be valued on a regular basis.

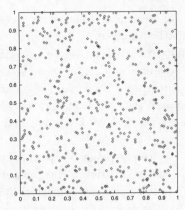

Fig. 4.1 512 pseudorandom points

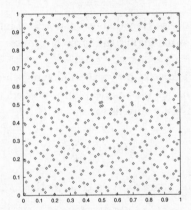

Fig. 4.2 512 low discrepancy points

Thus performance with a small number of points is particularly important for this class of applications. Contrast Figure 4.1, which exhibits 512 pseudorandom points, with Figure 4.2, which exhibits 512 low discrepancy points.

A software system called FINDER for computing high-dimensional integrals has been built at Columbia University. FINDER has modules for generating generalized Faure points and modified Sobol' points. As further improvements in low discrepancy methods are found, they will be added to the software. FINDER may be obtained from Columbia University.

Tests by other researchers, including Joy *et al.* [1996] and Ninomiya

& Tezuka [1996], lead to similar conclusions for the high-dimensional problems of mathematical finance.

The excellent results reported above are empirical. A number of hypotheses have been advanced to explain the observed results. For example, Caflisch *et al.* [1997] use a Brownian bridge argument to infer that the effective dimension of the CMO is much lower than its stated dimension. Another concept of effective dimension may be found in Paskov [1997].

We will discuss a very recent paper by Sloan & Woźniakowski [1998b], which might provide an explanation. Their paper is based on the observation that many problems of mathematical finance are highly non-isotropic. Assume that the various dimensions have "weights" $\gamma_1, \ldots, \gamma_d$, where

$$1 = \gamma_1 \geq \gamma_2 \geq \ldots \geq \gamma_d \geq 0.$$

For any such sequence γ, they define a class F_γ of integrands. (Note that this is an instance of changing the class of inputs, which was discussed in Chapter 3.)

Sloan and Woźniakowski prove the following theorem. Let $n(d, \gamma, \varepsilon)$ be the minimal number of sample points needed to reduce the initial error by a factor of ε, for any integrand in F_γ. If

$$s(d, \gamma) = \sum_{j=1}^{d} \gamma_j$$

is finite and "small," there exists a QMC method such that

$$n(d, \gamma, \varepsilon) \leq C\varepsilon^{-p} \qquad \text{for all } d, \qquad (4.4)$$

where C and p are constants, with $p \leq 2$. Note that unlike the stochastic guarantee of MC, this theorem offers a worst case guarantee.

Remark: For d finite and fixed, $s(d, \gamma)$ is, of course, finite. However, d is permitted to be arbitrarily large and, indeed, to go to infinity. □

The Sloan-Woźniakowski paper leaves a number of issues unresolved. The theorem of Sloan and Woźniakowski is about a class of integrands. To show that this explains why QMC methods are so effective for problems in finance, it has to be established that these problems have integrands belonging to F_γ.

The proof of (4.4) is nonconstructive. It is of a great practical importance to construct sample points for which (4.4) holds. It is hoped that known low discrepancy points satisfy (4.4). Furthermore, it is known that $p \leq 2$. If it could be shown that $p < 2$, then QMC, with a worst case guarantee, would beat MC. If it could be shown that p is close to 1, this would explain the empirical results from mathematical finance.

We summarize the discussion above by

Open Problems:
▷ Which financial problems have integrands belonging to F_γ?
▷ Provide a *deterministic* construction of a strongly tractable QMC method for F_γ.
▷ What is the best value of the exponent p in (4.4)?

Research into why QMC performs so well for high-dimensional integrals of mathematical finance is currently a very active area.

QMC looks promising for problems besides those occurring in mathematical finance. For example, Papageorgiou & Traub [1997] reported test results on the model integration problem (suggested by Keister [1996])

$$\left(\frac{1}{2\pi}\right)^{d/2} \int_{\mathbb{R}^d} \cos(\|x\|)e^{-\|x\|^2}\, dx, \tag{4.5}$$

where $\|\cdot\|$ denotes the Euclidean norm and $d = 25$. This problem is of particular interest, since it is isotropic, as opposed to the integrands of the finance problems, which are non-isotropic. The performance of the QMC-GF algorithm is very impressive. It achieved error 10^{-2} using fewer than 500 points. Its error over the range tested (up to 10^6 points) was $C \cdot n^{-1}$, with $C < 30$. By comparison, the error of the MC algorithm was proportional to $n^{-1/2}$. Although Keister [1996] stopped at $d = 25$, Papageorgiou & Traub [1997] tested (4.5) for dimension as high as 100, with results similar to those for $d = 25$.

There exists a transformation that reduces (4.5) to a univariate problem. The empirical convergence rate of QMC is n^{-1}, as if it sees that this is really a one-dimensional problem. In contrast, the empirical convergence rate of MC remains proportional to $n^{-1/2}$; it does not see that the problem is really one-dimensional. An analysis by Papageorgiou [1998] shows that an upper bound on the convergence rate of QMC is of order $n^{-1}(\log n)^{1/2}$.

These test results suggest that non-isotropicity is not the only condition under which QMC is superior to MC. Our current belief is that there are a number of classes of integrands for which QMC is superior to MC.

We end this chapter by summarizing its main points. We began with the Koksma-Hlawka and Woźniakowski theorems, which state that (modulo a polylog factor) QMC algorithms converge as n^{-1}, while MC converges as $n^{-1/2}$. These theorems make QMC appear to be a very promising alternative to MC. However, these theorems are for the asymptotic case; they say nothing about the kinds of problems one must solve in areas such as mathematical finance, where d is very large and the typical values of n are very much not "asymptotic." But the empirical results indicate that QMC is markedly superior to MC for many problems of mathematical finance. The theory should be enriched to explain the test results. We pose the following

Open Problem: Characterize classes of integrands for which QMC is superior to MC.

5

Complexity of Path Integration

Numerical integration has long been a fruitful source of problems in IBC. We discussed univariate and multivariate integration in Chapters 2 and 3. What can we say about integration for functions depending on an *infinite* number of variables? That is, we wish to approximate integrals of the form

$$S(f) = \int_X f(x)\, \mu(dx) \qquad \forall f \in F,$$

where μ is a probability measure on an infinite-dimensional space X and F is a class of functions f defined on X. This is usually called *path integration* or *functional integration*. The former name emphasizes that the most typical case is that of integration (with respect to Wiener measure) over continuous functions (or paths); the latter emphasizes that we integrate over a class of functions.

These infinite-dimensional problems are not merely of theoretical interest. Path integrals appear in many areas. Examples include

- quantum physics and chemistry,
- financial mathematics,
- the solution of partial differential equations.

For further discussion, examples, and references, see the introduction to Wasilkowski & Woźniakowski [1996].

The usual method for computing a path integral consists of

(i) approximating the original infinite-dimensional integral by one of finite dimension d, and then
(ii) using Monte Carlo to solve the d-dimensional integral.

From Chapter 3, we see that the second step yields an ε-approximation (in the randomized setting) to the d-dimensional integral, using $\Theta(\varepsilon^{-2})$

operations. Of course, to get an ε-approximation to the original problem, d may have to be huge; however, the number of function evaluations is independent of d. So the good news is that this approach gives us an ε-approximation. The bad news is that this approximation requires $\Theta(\varepsilon^{-2})$ function evaluations, which is expensive for small values of ε; moreover, we have only a stochastic guarantee of the quality of our answer since we are using the Monte Carlo method. Clearly we would be much happier with a worst case guarantee.

Can we do better? Is path integration *tractable* in the *worst case* setting, i.e., is the (worst case) ε-complexity at most $Kc\varepsilon^{-p}$ for some fixed p and K (where c is the cost of one evaluation of f or one of its derivatives)? We would be still happier if we could show that the problem is tractable with exponent less than 2, for then we would beat the usual algorithm on two fronts. Indeed, if this were so, then not only would we have a worst case (rather than stochastic) guarantee, but we would also know that there exists an algorithm whose cost is less than Monte Carlo.

The complexity of path integration is studied by Wasilkowski and Woźniakowski [1996]. They assume that μ is a Gaussian measure. Not surprisingly, the tractability of path integration depends on the regularity of the class F of problem elements.

First suppose that F is a class of f having finite regularity. More precisely, the class F consists of all functions $f: X \to \mathbb{R}$ whose rth Fréchet derivative $f^{(r)}$ is continuous, with $\max_{0 \le j \le r} \sup_{x \in X} \|f^{(j)}(x)\| \le 1$. If $r = 0$ or if the covariance operator C_μ of the Gaussian measure μ has infinite rank, then the path integration problem is intractable. However, if $r \ge 1$ and C_μ is of rank k, then the complexity is of order $c\varepsilon^{-k/r}$. Hence, the problem is tractable, with exponent k/r in this latter case.

Of course, a measure whose covariance operator has finite rank violates the spirit of path integration. After all, such a measure tells us that only a finite number of dimensions really matters in our infinite-dimensional domain X. Moreover, the most commonly used Gaussian measure is the Wiener measure, whose correlation operator is of infinite rank. So the result in the previous paragraph tells us that if we only consider interesting measures, then the path integration problem is intractable (in the worst case setting) for problem elements having finite smoothness.

Since the path integration problem is intractable in the worst case setting for integrands having finite regularity, Wasilkowski and Woźniakowski next investigated tractability in the randomized setting. Suppose that the nth eigenvalue of C_μ decreases no faster than polynomially in n. (For instance, this holds for the Wiener measure, where the nth eigenvalue is proportional to n^{-2}.) Then the randomized complexity is $\Theta(c\varepsilon^{-2})$. Since the Monte Carlo algorithm costs $(c+1)\varepsilon^{-2}$ and yields an approximation whose expected error is at most ε, we see that Monte Carlo is essentially optimal, *no matter what finite value r has*.

In summary, for problem classes having finite regularity, path integration is intractable in the worst case setting. However, the problem is tractable in the randomized setting, and Monte Carlo is essentially optimal.

We have just seen that path integration is intractable for problems of finite smoothness in the worst case setting. What happens when functions in F have infinite smoothness? Wasilkowski and Woźniakowski consider particular classes F of entire functions. For such classes, they construct an algorithm for calculating a worst case ε-approximation with worst case cost at most $Kc\varepsilon^{-p}$, where the exponent p depends on the Gaussian measure μ. They show that $p \le 2$ always holds, and that if the nth eigenvalue of C_μ is proportional to n^{-s}, then $p = 2/(2s-1)$. In particular, for the Wiener measure, they found $p = \frac{2}{3}$.

Since $p \le 2$, this new algorithm (with a worst case assurance) never needs more evaluations than the Monte Carlo algorithm (with a randomized assurance). However, this is not an entirely fair comparison:

(i) Monte Carlo is applicable for a much wider class of functions. More precisely, Monte Carlo is well-defined (and its randomized error bound holds) for continuous functions in the L_2 unit ball, whereas the algorithm of Wasilkowski and Woźniakowski is only defined for a class of entire functions.

(ii) Monte Carlo uses only function evaluations, whereas the new algorithm uses evaluations of the integrand and its derivatives at the origin (somewhat like a Taylor series). If these derivatives are unavailable, then the new algorithm is no longer admissible.

The study of complexity and algorithms for path integration is a rich area for further research. An important example is the famous Feynman-Kac integral, which gives the solution of the heat equation, see, e.g., Chorin [1973] and Hald [1987]. Plaskota *et al.* [1998] study the complexity of Feynman-Kac path integrals.

Note that complexity results are available for functions with finite regularity. However, we know only an upper bound on the complexity for entire functions. We pose two

Open Problems:

▷ What is the complexity of path integration for entire functions in the worst case setting? Is the algorithm of Wasilkowski and Woźniakowski essentially optimal?

▷ What is the complexity of path integration for entire functions in the randomized setting?

6

Are Ill-Posed Problems Solvable?

Pour-El & Richards [1988] have shown that there are partial differential equations with computable initial conditions and non-computable solutions. Examples include the backwards heat equation and the wave equation with non-smooth initial conditions. Their result has stirred considerable interest; see, for example, Penrose [1989] and Barrow [1990].

These results concerning partial differential equations are a special case of their general theorem, which states that a linear unbounded transformation causes non-computability. The Pour-El and Richards work is done in the context of *computability theory*, and this theorem is the main result of their monograph.

Independently, Werschulz [1987b] obtained an analogous conclusion regarding unbounded transformations in the context of *information-based complexity*. In contrast to Pour-El and Richards, his proof takes about a page.

The theorems above are for the worst case setting. In IBC, it is natural to also consider the average case setting. Here, there is a very surprising result which we describe below.

It will be most convenient to describe these results using the terminology of ill-posed problems. In a seminal paper, Hadamard [1902] developed the notion of a "correctly set," or *well-posed*, problem as being one for which the solution operator S is continuous. Thus for a well-posed problem, a small change in the problem element f produces a small change in the solution element $S(f)$. A problem that is not well-posed is said to be *ill-posed*. As one can infer from his terminology, Hadamard felt that there was something inherently wrong with trying to solve ill-posed problems. Given an ill-posed problem, one should attempt to reformulate it, so that it can be correctly set. This issue is dealt with at length in the treatise Hadamard [1952].

However, there are many important ill-posed problems that occur in practice, such as remote sensing and computational vision. See Section 6.4 of Werschulz [1991] for further discussion and references.

Can we solve ill-posed problems? We distinguish between three levels of solvability:

(i) The problem is *solvable* if we can compute an ε-approximation for any $\varepsilon > 0$, no matter how small.

(ii) The problem is *weakly solvable* if there exists an $\varepsilon_0 > 0$ such that we can compute an ε-approximation iff $\varepsilon \geq \varepsilon_0$.

(iii) The problem is *unsolvable* if we cannot compute an ε-approximation, no matter how large we choose ε to be.

We restrict our attention to solution operators that are linear transformations S of normed linear spaces. It is well-known that S is continuous iff it is *bounded*, i.e., if

$$\sup_{f \in F} \|S(f)\| < \infty,$$

where

$$F = \{\, f \in D : \|f\| \leq 1 \,\} \tag{6.1}$$

and D is the domain of S. Thus a linear problem is well-posed if S is bounded, and ill-posed if S is unbounded.

We first consider the worst case setting. Our class F of problem elements is given by (6.1). Werschulz [1987b] proved that if S is unbounded, then we have

$$e^{\mathrm{wor}}(\phi, N) = \infty$$

for any information N of finite cardinality and any algorithm ϕ using N. In other words, no algorithm using partial information can compute an approximation having finite error. Clearly, this means that

$$\mathrm{comp}^{\mathrm{wor}}(\varepsilon) = \infty \qquad \forall \varepsilon \geq 0.$$

Thus ill-posed problems are unsolvable in the worst case setting.

We must switch to a different setting if we are to solve ill-posed problems. Since ill-posed problems are unsolvable in the worst case setting, one might hope that positive results can be achieved by going to the average case setting, and introducing a concept of being "well-posed on the average."

We say that a linear operator S is *bounded on the average* if

$$\int_D \|S(f)\|^2 \, \mu(df) < \infty.$$

(Of course, there are a number of technical requirements on the domain D of S and the probability measure μ that must hold if this integral is to be well-defined; see Werschulz [1987b] for the details.) Then a problem is *well-posed on the average* if S is bounded on the average, and is *ill-posed on the average* if S is not bounded on the average.

It turns out that when the problem is well-posed on the average, it is solvable in the average case setting. However, when the problem is ill-posed on the average, it can be solvable, weakly solvable, or unsolvable in the average case setting, depending on the measure μ, see Traub & Werschulz [1994].

Suppose now that μ is a Gaussian measure. Werschulz [1987b] showed that the problem is solvable in the average case setting iff it is bounded on the average. It is natural to seek a linear ill-posed problem that is also ill-posed on the average. After repeated attempts to do this failed, it was conjectured that every measurable unbounded linear operator is bounded on the average, for all Gaussian measures. This was proven independently by Kon *et al.* [1991] and Vakhania [1991]. The following rather remarkable theorem follows. *Every linear ill-posed problem is solvable on the average, for all Gaussian measures.* (However, such a problem may still be intractable in the sense of Chapter 3.) For an expository account, see Traub & Werschulz [1994].

We close this section by presenting an open problem. Recall the main result of Pour-El & Richards [1988], namely, that an unbounded linear transformation is non-computable. This is a result of computability theory. On the other hand, there are two major results in IBC about the complexity of problems defined by linear transformations:

(i) *Worst case setting*: If the transformation is unbounded, the problem is unsolvable.

(ii) *Average case setting, Gaussian measure*: The problem is solvable (assuming only that the transformation is measurable).

Result (i) has an analog in computability theory. However, while there has been some work on computability on the average (see, e.g., Ben-David *et al.* [1992]), there is no computability-theoretic analog to result (ii). Hence, we pose the following

Open Problem: Is every (measurable) linear operator computable on the average for Gaussian measures?

7

Complexity of Nonlinear Problems

The vast majority of the material presented so far has dealt with the complexity of linear problems. This is because we have been able to develop a coherent framework to study general linear problems in a variety of settings. When it comes to nonlinear problems, however, there is little general theory.

There is a difference in kind between nonlinear problems and linear problems. *Nonlinearity is not a property—it is the lack of a property.* This means that nonlinear problems must be dealt with on a case-by-case basis, since different nonlinear problems will generally have little in common with each other.

The early roots of IBC dealt with both linear (Sard [1949], Nikolskij [1950]) and nonlinear (Kiefer [1953], Traub [1961], [1964]) problems. Most of the work on the complexity of nonlinear problems dealt with the asymptotic or worst case complexity of solving nonlinear equations (see, e.g., Section B of Traub and Woźniakowski [1980] and the relevant sections in Traub *et al.* [1988]).

There has also been work on the complexity of nonlinear problems arising from the solution of linear operator equations. Here, we wish to solve problems of the form $Lu = f$, with L a linear differential or integral operator depending on coefficient functions. The nonlinearity arises when we have partial information about the coefficient functions, as well as about the right-hand side function f. Research in this area can be traced back at least as far as Emelyanov & Ilin [1967], who studied the complexity of Fredholm problems of the second kind; see also the relevant portions of Werschulz [1991].

All this research on the complexity of nonlinear problems had been in the asymptotic or worst case settings. It is only recently that the

61

complexity of nonlinear problems has been studied in other settings. We report on recent results for two problems.

Other important lines of work that we won't describe here include the complexity of fixed-point iterations (Hirsch *et al.* [1989], Sikorski and Woźniakowski [1987], Vavasis [1991]) and nonlinear optimization (Calvin [1997], Nemirovsky & Nesterov [1994], Nemirovsky & Yudin [1983], Wasilkowski [1992c]).

7.1 The Fredholm Problem of the Second Kind

Consider the solution u to the Fredholm problem of the second kind

$$u(x) - \int_{[0,1]^d} k(x,y)u(y)\,dy = f(x) \qquad \forall\, x \in [0,1]^d \qquad (7.1)$$

at a fixed, but arbitrary, point $x_0 \in [0,1]^d$. Suppose that we have partial information on both the kernel k and the right-hand side f; then the solution operator mapping (k,f) onto $u(x_0)$ is nonlinear. This problem was studied in the worst case setting by Emelyanov & Ilin [1967]. Suppose that the kernel k and the right-hand side f belong to balls in C^r. Then the nth minimal radius is $\Theta(n^{-r/(2d)})$, and comp$(\varepsilon) = \Theta(\varepsilon^{-2d/r})$.

Heinrich & Mathé [1993] studied this problem in the randomized setting. They showed that the nth minimal randomized error is proportional to $n^{-(r/(2d)+1/2)}$, and that the ε-complexity is proportional to $\varepsilon^{-2d/(r+d)}$. Thus this problem suffers from the curse of dimensionality in the worst case setting, but the curse is broken in the randomized setting.

Note that the nth randomized minimal radius is the product of two factors. The first is $\Theta(n^{-r/(2d)})$, which is the worst case minimal radius for the Fredholm problem; the second is $\Theta(n^{-1/2})$, the randomized minimal radius for the integration problem with continuous integrands. So it will come as no surprise to learn that the optimal algorithm they suggest has both a deterministic and a stochastic part. More precisely, they start out with an optimal deterministic method to produce a first approximation v to the exact solution u. Let

$$g = v - \int_{[0,1]^d} h(\cdot,y)v(y)\,dy$$

where h is a finite element approximation of k. Define a random variable

$$\tilde{\eta}_\tau(k,f) = v(t_0) + \eta_\tau(k,f) - \eta_\tau(h,g),$$

where η_τ is the random variable that arises in the classical von Neumann-Ulam Monte Carlo scheme to approximate solutions of second-kind Fredholm problems. It is easy to see that $u(x_0)$ is the expected value of $\tilde{\eta}_\tau(k, f)$. This algorithm consists of n independent realizations of $\tilde{\eta}_\tau$. Since the square root of the variance of $\tilde{\eta}_\tau(k, f)$ is $\Theta(n^{-r/(2d)})$ and the standard Monte Carlo contribution is $\Theta(n^{-1/2})$, we see that the error of this algorithm is $\Theta(n^{-(r/(2d)+1/2)})$. This algorithm is optimal, since Heinrich and Mathé also established a matching lower bound on the nth minimal error.

Further discussion of optimal algorithms for the Fredholm problem of the second kind may be found in the monographs Frank [1997] and Pereverzev [1996], both of which include extensive bibliographies.

7.2 Nonlinear Equations

Let F be a subset of the class of continuous functions on a compact interval that change signs at the endpoints of that interval. We are interested in obtaining approximate solutions of the nonlinear equation $f(x) = 0$, for $f \in F$.

Sikorski [1985] surveyed worst case complexity for nonlinear equations. A typical result is that the bisection method is an optimal algorithm for many such classes F, so that $\mathrm{comp}^{\mathrm{wor}}(\varepsilon) = \Theta(\log(1/\varepsilon))$. To what extent do these results hold in the average case setting? That is, we want to know whether bisection is always optimal on the average, and whether we can do zero-finding significantly faster in the average case setting.

We first address the optimality of bisection. Graf *et al.* [1989] showed that bisection is not always optimal on the average. The problem elements are a class of monotone functions, under the Ulam measure. They found that there is a strategy that reduces the average interval of uncertainty by a factor of about 0.49 at each step. Hence their strategy is a little bit better than bisection, which only reduces the average uncertainty by a factor of 0.5 per step.

Of course, the improvement given by the strategy in Graf *et al.* [1989] over bisection is slight. Are there methods that do significantly better on the average than bisection? The answer to this question depends crucially on whether an adaptive stopping rule is used.

Suppose first that the number of evaluations is fixed in advance. Novak & Ritter [1993] showed that $\mathrm{comp}^{\mathrm{avg}}(\varepsilon) = \Theta(\log(1/\varepsilon))$ for continuous functions changing sign at the endpoints, equipped with the Brownian bridge measure. This result was extended to classes of C^r-functions equipped with a conditional r-fold Wiener measure (with $r \geq 0$) and to classes of monotone functions equipped with the Ulam measure by Ritter [1994]. Hence, bisection is optimal (to within a multiplicative constant) on the average if the number of evaluations is fixed in advance.

On the other hand, suppose that we now allow adaptive stopping rules. Novak *et al.* [1995] showed that if $r \geq 2$, then $\mathrm{comp}^{\mathrm{avg}}(\varepsilon) = \Theta(\log \log(1/\varepsilon))$. (This is the kind of cost we expect from Newton iterations. But note that Newton requires derivatives, whereas there are no derivative evaluations here. Moreover, we *are* using two different settings!) The optimal algorithm is a simple modification of the well-known hybrid secant-bisection method. Thus

(i) adaptive stopping is exponentially better than nonadaptive stopping, and

(ii) if adaptive stopping is allowed, bisection is exponentially nonoptimal.

8

What Model of Computation Should Be Used by Scientists?

A central dogma of computer science is that the Turing machine is *the* appropriate abstraction of a computer. We discuss whether it is the appropriate abstraction when a digital computer is used for scientific computation.

First, we introduce the four "worlds" that will play a role; see Table 8.1. Above the horizontal line are two real worlds: the world of physical phenomena and the computer world in which simulations are performed. Below the horizontal line are two formal models: a mathematical model of a real-world phenomenon and a model of computation that is an abstraction of a physical computer. A real-world phenomenon can be a natural phenomenon (such as the weather) or an artificial phenomenon (such as the course of interest rates). *We get to choose both the mathematical model and the model of computation. What type of models should we choose?*

Table 8.1. *Four worlds*

Real-world phenomena	Computer simulation
Mathematical model	Model of computation

The mathematical model, which is often continuous, is chosen by the scientist. Continuous models are common in disciplines ranging from physics to economics. The real or complex number field is *assumed*. For simplicity, we refer only to the reals in what follows. It is well-understood that the real numbers are an abstraction. That is, it would take an infinite number of bits to explicitly represent a single real number; an infinite number of bits is not available in the universe. Real numbers are utilized because they are a powerful and useful construct.

65

But the computer is a finite state machine. *What should we do when the continuous mathematical model meets the finite state machine?* We compare and contrast two models of computation: the Turing machine model and the real-number model.† In the interest of full disclosure, we've always used the real-number model in our work, but will do our best to present balanced arguments. We will assume the reader is familiar with the Turing machine as an abstraction of a digital computer. Turing [1937] was one of the intellectual giants of the twentieth century, who defined this machine model to establish the unsolvability of Hilbert's *Entscheidungsproblem*. In the real-number model, we assume that we can store and perform arithmetic operations and comparisons on real numbers exactly and at unit cost. Of course, this is an abstraction and the test is how useful and close to reality the abstraction is.

The real-number model has a long history. Ostrowski [1954] used it in his work on the computational complexity of polynomial evaluation. Traub [1964] used the real-number model for research on optimal iteration theory. Winograd [1967] and Strassen [1969] used the real-number model in their work on algebraic complexity in the late 1960s. Traub & Woźniakowski [1980] used it in their monograph on information-based complexity. Blum *et al.* [1989] provided a formalization of the real-number model for continuous combinatorial complexity, and established the existence of NP-complete problems over the reals. Their paper led to a surge of research on computation over the reals.

What are the pros and cons for these two models of computation? We'll begin with the pros of the Turing machine model. It is desirable to use a finite state abstraction of a finite state machine. Moreover, the Turing machine's simplicity and economy of description are attractive. Another plus is that it is universal. It is universal in two senses. The first is the *Church-Turing hypothesis*, which states that what a Turing machine can compute may be considered a universal definition of computability. (Computability on a Turing machine is equivalent to computability in Church's lambda calculus.) Of course, one cannot prove this thesis; it appeals to our intuitive notion of computability. It is universal in a second sense. All "reasonable" machines are polynomially equivalent to Turing machines. Informally, this means that if the minimal time to compute an output on a Turing machine is $T(n)$ for an input of size n and if the minimal time to compute an output on any

---

† Other models of computation have been considered. See the papers in Calude *et al.* [1998] and their extensive bibliographies for discussions of models of computation appropriate for quantum and DNA computing.

Table 8.2. *Pros of the Turing machine model*

- Desirable to use finite state model for finite state machine
- Universal
  - Church-Turing thesis
  - All "reasonable" machines are polynomially equivalent to Turing machines

---

other machine is $S(n)$, then $T(n)$ and $S(n)$ are polynomially related. Therefore, one might as well use the Turing machine as the model of computation.

We're not convinced by the assertion that all reasonable machines are polynomially equivalent to Turing machines, but will defer this critique to our consideration of the cons of the Turing machine. See Table 8.2 for a summary of the pros of the Turing machine model.

We turn to the cons of the Turing machine model. We believe it is not natural to use this discrete model in conjunction with continuous mathematical models. Furthermore, estimated running times on a Turing machine are not predictive of scientific computation on digital computers. One reason for this is that scientific computation is usually done with fixed-precision floating point arithmetic. The cost of arithmetic operations is independent of the size of the operands. Turing machine operations depend on number size.

Finally, there are interesting models that are not polynomially equivalent to a Turing machine. Consider the example of a UMRAM, i.e., a Random Access Machine where Multiplication is a basic operation, and memory access and the operations of multiplication and addition can be performed at Unit cost. This seems like a reasonable abstraction of a digital computer, since multiplication and addition on fixed-precision floating point numbers cost about the same. But the UMRAM is *not* polynomially equivalent to a Turing machine! (See, e.g., p. 25 in van Emde Boas [1990].) However, a RAM, which does not have multiplication as a fundamental operation, *is* polynomially equivalent to a Turing machine. The cons of the Turing machine model are summarized in Table 8.3.

We turn to the pros of the real-number model. As stated above, mathematical models are often continuous and use real (or complex) numbers. That is, a continuum is *assumed*. It seems natural to us to use the real numbers in analyzing the numerical solution of continuous

Table 8.3. *Cons of the Turing machine model*

- Not natural to use a discrete model of computation in conjunction with the continuous models of science
- Not predictive of running time of scientific computation on a digital computer
- Not all "reasonable" machines are equivalent to Turing machines

---

models on a digital computer. We believe that a Turing machine model would not be natural.

Most scientific computation uses fixed-precision floating point arithmetic. Modulo stability, computational complexity in the real-number model is the same as for fixed-precision floating point. Therefore, the real-number model is predictive of running times for scientific computation.

A third reason for using the real-number model is that it permits the full power of continuous mathematics. Consider, for example, ill-posed problems, which were discussed in Chapter 6. There is an important unsolvability result about ill-posed problems, in both the Turing machine and real-number models. The Turing machine version of this result takes a substantial part of a monograph to prove. With analysis, the analogous result in the real-number model takes about a page.

The argument for using the power of analysis was already made in 1948 by John von Neumann, one of the scientific giants of the century and a father of the digital computer. In his Hixon Symposium lecture (von Neumann [1961], see also the discussion in Blum *et al.* [1998]), he argues for a "more specifically analytical theory of automata and of information." He writes:

There exists today a very elaborate system of formal logic, and specifically, of logic as applied to mathematics. This is a discipline with many good sides, but also serious weaknesses.... Everybody who has worked in formal logic will confirm that it is one of the technically most refractory parts of mathematics. The reason for this is that it deals with rigid, all-or-none concepts, and has very little contact with the continuous concept of the real or of the complex number, that is, with mathematical analysis. Yet analysis is the technically most successful and best-elaborated part of mathematics. ... The theory of automata, of the digital, all-or-none type as discussed up to now, is certainly a chapter in formal logic. It would, therefore, seem that it will have to share this unattractive property of formal logic.

Table 8.4. *Pros of the real-number model*

- "Natural" for continuous mathematical models
- Predictive of computer performance on scientific problems
- Utilizes the power of continuous mathematics

Table 8.5. *Cons of the real-number model*

- It is impossible to construct a physical device that implements the real-number model.
- It is preferable to use a finite state abstraction of a finite state machine.

These observations may be used *mutatis mutandis* as an argument for the real-number model.

Blum *et al.* [1998] argue for the real-number model, saying, "The point of view of this book is that the Turing model ... is fundamentally inadequate for giving such a foundation to the theory of modern scientific computation, where most of the algorithms ... are *real-number algorithms*." The pros of the real-number model are summarized in Table 8.4.

A con of the real-number model is that the digital representation of real numbers does not exist in the real world. Even a single real number would require infinite resources to represent exactly. Thus the real-number model is not finitistic. The Turing machine is also not finitistic, since it utilizes an unbounded tape. It is therefore *potentially* infinite. Thus, to paraphrase George Orwell, the real-number model is more infinite than the Turing machine model. It would be attractive to have a completely finite model of computation. There are finite models, such as circuit models and linear bounded automata, but they are special-purpose. The cons of the real-number model are summarized in Table 8.5.

9

Do Impossibility Theorems from Formal Models Limit Scientific Knowledge?

Starting with the seminal papers of Gödel [1931] and Turing [1937], this century has witnessed a stream of impossibility results, including *undecidability*, *non-computability*, and *intractability*. But these results concern formal models. Do they limit scientific knowledge? We will discuss the implications of these three impossibility results for scientific knowledge.

Do *undecidability* results, such as those of Gödel [1931], Turing [1937], and Chaitin [1988], set intrinsic limits to scientific knowledge? Many people seem to think so. One of us (JFT) once mentioned to a very senior European physicist that he was interested in understanding intrinsic limits to scientific knowledge; the physicist replied that such intrinsic limits had been established by Gödel.

This is not so. Gödel's incompleteness theorem concerns formal systems. He showed that if a system as rich as arithmetic is consistent, it cannot be complete. That is, there are statements in the system that cannot be proved true or false within the system; arithmetic is *undecidable*.

A scientific question does not come equipped with a mathematical model. Here are some examples of scientific questions:

- Why do the ratios of the masses of the elementary particles have their particular values?
- Can the average healthy, active life-span of humans be significantly prolonged by (say) a factor of 2 or 3?
- How did life originate on earth?
- Will the universe expand forever, or will it collapse?
- How do physical processes in the brain give rise to subjective experience?

- How do children acquire language?

Gödel's theorem cannot be used directly to answer any of these questions. Nor can it be used more generally to infer a limit to scientific knowledge. This is for a number of reasons. The first is that there might be something special about the mathematical models describing nature that makes them decidable. Secondly, the mathematical models are not unique. Scientists seek models that capture the essence of the phenomenon under study. Within this constraint, the scientist is free to choose. Therefore, Gödel's theorem might set limits to scientific knowledge if every mathematical statement that captures the essence of a phenomenon is undecidable.

This last observation suggests how undecidability theorems of formal systems might be used to prove limits to scientific knowledge, see Traub [1991]. Consider all mathematical models that capture the essence of a scientific question, and prove that each of them is undecidable. This may be a possible attack in principle, but it is far from evident that it could actually be carried out for any non-trivial question. An alternative attack is suggested in Traub [1997]. We have the

---

Open Problem: Does Gödel's theorem limit scientific knowledge?

Even if a mathematical model is decidable within a certain formal system, the computational resources required for its solution may not be available in principle if the model is intractable. Can *intractability* results be used to infer limits to scientific knowledge?

The argument is similar to the discussion above on Gödel's theorem. For a scientific question, we get to choose the mathematical model. To rigorously demonstrate an impassable barrier due to intractability, we should show that *all* mathematical models capturing the essence of a scientific question are intractable. As before, this may be a possible attack in principle, but it is far from evident that it could actually be carried out for any non-trivial question. Note, however, that in establishing the computational complexity of a mathematical model, we do permit *all* possible algorithms to compete.

Open Problem: Do intractability theorems limit scientific knowledge?

We turn to a third kind of negative result—*non-computability*. Recall that a number is *computable* if there is a mechanical procedure for approximating it to arbitrary precision; see, for example, Turing [1937]

or Geroch & Hartle [1986]. An example of a computable number is π. However, almost all real numbers are non-computable. A number of scientists have expressed surprise and concern about non-computable numbers. Geroch & Hartle [1986] ask whether the occurrence of a non-computable, but measurable, number in a physical theory indicates a difficulty with the theory. Penrose [1989] is concerned by the result that the wave equation with computable initial conditions can have non-computable solutions; he calls this a "rather startling result." Faced with the same result, Barrow [1990] concludes: "The answer to these difficulties, if they can be found, surely lies in an enlarged concept of what we mean by a computation." In addition, a number of physicists have told us of their unease.

It seems to us that there are two issues with respect to non-computable numbers in physics:

- Are they impediments to comparing experiment with theory?
- Does it indicate a flaw in a physical theory if measurable observables are non-computable?

First consider the question of agreement of theoretical predictions with experiment. Although experimental results are known to only limited accuracy, computability is an asymptotic concept. Non-computability does not affect any fixed finite number of digits.

What *does* matter in drawing conclusions from theoretical models is the cost of computing the ith digit. Assume, for example, that computing the ith digit of x costs 10^{10i} operations. We will never be able to compute more than the first few digits of x, even if x is a computable number. Thus the costs of algorithms, rather than non-computability, may be the fundamental impediment to comparing theory with experiment.

To illuminate the second question, we discuss several examples. First, consider Geroch & Hartle [1986]. They define measurability and computability very generally, and then consider a particular observable in quantum gravity. They present arguments suggesting that a certain observable may be non-computable. They also discuss why they are quite far from *proving* that this observable is non-computable.

Next, consider partial differential equations with computable initial conditions but non-computable solutions. The equations are very simple. Examples are the wave equation and the backwards heat equation. The wave equation is assumed to have initial conditions that are not twice differentiable. These partial differential equations are special cases of *ill-posed problems*, which are discussed at greater length in Chapter 6. M. B. Pour-El and J. Richards have expended considerable effort investigating computability and ill-posed problems. They showed that if a problem is ill-posed, then there always exists a computable input that is mapped to a non-computable output. Thus, ill-posed problems are a source of non-computability. Does this imply a limit about what we can know about scientific problems governed by ill-posed mathematical models?

One of us (AGW) has investigated the *solvability* of ill-posed problems, see Chapter 6. In the worst case, such problems are unsolvable; that is, it is impossible to compute an ε-approximation at finite cost, even for arbitrarily large ε. However, in the average case setting with respect to any Gaussian measure, *all linear ill-posed problems are solvable*. We see that the non-solvability of ill-posed problems is a worst case phenomenon. It melts away in the average case for Gaussian measures.

We pose a third

> *Open Problem*: Do non-computability results limit scientific knowledge?

We've not seen convincing evidence that the answer is "yes."

10
Complexity of Linear Programming

We'll use the complexity of linear programming (LP) to illustrate the dependence of complexity results on the model of computation. As we'll see, although the complexity of LP is polynomial in the Turing machine model, the question of its complexity in the real-number model is open.

Khachian [1979] studied an ellipsoid algorithm and proved that LP is polynomial (and therefore, by definition, tractable) in the Turing machine model. Traub and Woźniakowski [1979] give a brief history of the work leading up to his result. Khachian's theorem caused enormous interest; an amusing account of the media coverage may be found in Lawler [1980]. However, Traub and Woźniakowski [1982] showed that the cost of this ellipsoid algorithm is not polynomial in the real-number model, and conjectured that the LP problem is not polynomial in the real-number model. (This nicely emphasizes the difference between the cost of an algorithm and the complexity of a problem, since the result concerning the cost of the ellipsoid algorithm leaves open the question of problem complexity.)

Although Khachian used the Turing machine model in his paper, it will be convenient to utilize a polynomially equivalent random access machine (RAM) in this chapter. Following Traub & Woźniakowski [1982], we make the following assumptions regarding the two models. In this chapter, "arithmetic operations" shall mean the usual operations of addition, subtraction, multiplication, division, and comparison, as well as the square root operation.

- Real-Number Model
  - Number system: reals
  - Arithmetic: exact
  - Cost: unit cost for each operation

- RAM model
  - Number system: integers
  - Arithmetic: exact or approximate
  - Cost: proportional to size of numbers (logarithmic cost)

Key to the discussion is the definition of polynomial complexity in each model. We will assume that $\varepsilon = 0$; that is, the problem is to be solved exactly. Let n be a measure of problem size in the real-number model. If the problem complexity is a polynomial in n, we say the problem has *polynomial complexity in the real-number model.*

In the RAM model, let L be the number of digits needed to represent the input. If the problem complexity is a polynomial in L, we say the problem has *polynomial complexity in the RAM model.* Thus the definition of polynomial complexity (and, therefore, of tractability) depends on the model of computation.

In related work, Megiddo [1983] defined "genuinely polynomial" and Tardos [1986] defined "strongly polynomial." Although Tardos obtained a partial result, the question of whether linear programming is strongly polynomial remains open.

To illustrate these concepts, we use the example of solving the linear system $Ax = y$, where A is a $k \times k$ nonsingular matrix.

Consider first the real-number model. The size of the problem is $n = k^2 + k$. Gaussian elimination costs $O(k^3)$ arithmetic operations. Hence the complexity of solving linear equalities in the real-number model is polynomial. (Since the complexity of linear equalities is the same as the complexity of matrix multiplication, the exponent is actually less than 3, but that need not concern us here.)

Consider next the RAM model. If b is the number of digits used to represent a single data item, then the total number of digits used to represent the data is $L = b \cdot (k^2 + k)$. There is an algorithm (Edmonds [1967]) such that the numerators and denominators of the solutions can be computed at cost which is polynomial in L. Hence the complexity of solving linear equalities is also polynomial in the RAM model.

Since LP can be reduced to the solution of linear inequalities, we will confine ourselves to examining the complexity of the latter. To be specific, suppose that we are solving a system of m linear inequalities in k variables. The size of the problem in the real-number model is $n = km + m$; in the RAM model, the number of digits needed to represent the data is $L = b \cdot (km + m)$.

As stated above, Khachian [1979] showed that the complexity is polynomial in the RAM model. However, Traub & Woźniakowski [1982] proved that the ellipsoid algorithm described in Khachian's paper is not polynomial in the real-number model. They did this by considering the problem of solving the 2×2 parameterized system $Ax < y$ of inequalities, where

$$A = \begin{pmatrix} 1 & 0 \\ -1 & 0 \end{pmatrix} \text{ and } y = \begin{pmatrix} 1 + s^{-1} \\ -1 \end{pmatrix}, \text{ with } s \geq \frac{5}{\sqrt{2}}.$$

They proved that the number of steps used by the ellipsoid algorithm grows as $\log s$, and is therefore unbounded as s increases.

Now assume that s is an integer. Multiplying by s yields inequalities with integer coefficients. Observe that $L \approx \log s$. Hence this little example shows that the number of steps required by the ellipsoid algorithm increases as L. Thus the ellipsoid algorithm is not polynomial in the real-number model. The same conclusion applies to interior-point methods, such as those of Karmarkar [1984] and Renegar [1988].

No known algorithm for solving inequalities is polynomial in the real-number model. Traub & Woźniakowski [1982] proposed two conjectures concerning the complexity of linear inequalities. Since they have not been settled, we propose them here as

---

Open Problems: Prove the following conjectures:
▷ The linear inequalities problem does not have polynomial complexity in the real-number model.
▷ The solution of linear inequalities is strictly harder than linear equalities in all reasonable models of computation.

11

Complexity of Verification

So far in this monograph, we have discussed the optimal *computation* of ε-approximations, which is the primary focus of information-based complexity. In this chapter and the next, we discuss two other tasks of IBC—verification and testing.

In *verification*, we are given a problem and a proposed answer, and asked to check whether the proposed answer is within ε of the true answer. Intuition suggests that checking is surely easier than computing; as we shall see, this intuition is incorrect.

We formalize this in the worst case setting. Suppose that $S \colon F \to G$ is our solution operator. Then for a problem element $f \in F$ and a given input element $g \in G$, we wish to determine whether

$$\|S(f) - g\| \leq \varepsilon.$$

We define the verification operator

$$\text{VER}(f, g) = \begin{cases} \text{YES} & \text{if } \|S(f) - g\| \leq \varepsilon, \\ \text{NO} & \text{if } \|S(f) - g\| > \varepsilon. \end{cases}$$

Since the answer is either YES or NO, we see that verification is a decision problem.

As with computation, we only have partial information $N_g(f) = N(f; g)$ about f; note that the information may also depend on g. This means that we can only compute approximations

$$U(f, g) = \phi(N(f; g), g)$$

to the verification operator, where $\phi \colon N(F \times G) \times G \to \{\text{YES}, \text{NO}\}$ is an algorithm and N is information of finite cardinality.

77

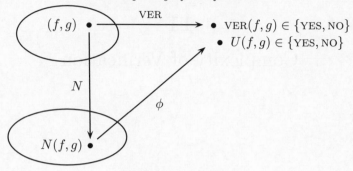

Fig. 11.1 Verification

Verification is represented by the diagram in Figure 11.1; this may be contrasted with Figure 2.2, which represents computation in IBC.

Note that if we can compute $S(f)$ exactly with finite cost, then we can verify a proposed solution with only two additional operations (a norm calculation and a comparison). So we can restrict our attention to problems for which exact solutions are not available at finite cost.

Under natural hypotheses, Woźniakowski [1992c] proved that verification is unsolvable in the worst case setting, even when the solution operator and information are linear. That is, there exists no approximation that always gives the correct answer for verification, even when the problem is linear. This holds, regardless of whether the information is adaptive or nonadaptive.

To provide the reader with some intuition regarding this surprising result, consider the following simple

Example: Let

$$F = \{\, [0,1] \xrightarrow{f} \mathbb{R} : \mathrm{Lip}(f) \leq 1 \,\},$$
$$G = \mathbb{R},$$
$$S(f) = \int_0^1 f(x)\, dx \qquad \forall f \in F,$$
$$N_g(f) = [f(x_1), \ldots, f(x_n)] \qquad \forall g \in \mathbb{R}.$$

We wish to verify proposed solutions to the integration problem for Lipschitz functions on the unit interval, our information being standard information (function values). Is a given number g an ε-approximation to the integral of a function f having Lipschitz constant at most one? Note that the sample points $x_1, \ldots, x_n$ may depend on g.

Consider what happens when $g = 0$. Suppose that $f \in F$ is a function

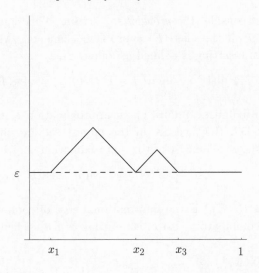

Fig. 11.2 Two functions sharing the same information for the verification problem

for which

$$f(x_i) = \varepsilon \qquad (1 \le i \le n). \tag{11.1}$$

We define two functions from F that are consistent with this data, see Figure 11.2. The first is the constant function $f_1 \equiv \varepsilon$, whereas the second is the piecewise-linear function f_2 interpolating the data points

$$\{(0, \varepsilon), (1, \varepsilon)\} \cup \{(x_i, \varepsilon)\}_{i=1}^{n} \cup \{(\tfrac{1}{2}(x_i + x_{i+1}), \varepsilon + \tfrac{1}{2}(x_{i+1} - x_i))\}_{i=1}^{n-1}.$$

Now let ϕ be an algorithm for solving our verification problem. Then either $\phi(N_g(f), g) = \text{YES}$ or $\phi(N_g(f), g) = \text{NO}$ for any f satisfying (11.1). Suppose first that $\phi(N_g(f), g) = \text{YES}$ for all such f. In particular, this means that $\phi(N_g(f_2), g) = \text{YES}$. But clearly $\int_0^1 f_2(x)\,dx > \varepsilon$, so that $|S(f_2) - g| > \varepsilon$, i.e., the YES answer produced by our algorithm is wrong. On the other hand, suppose that $\phi(N_g(f), g) = \text{NO}$ for all such f, implying that $\phi(N_g(f_1), g) = \text{NO}$. But $\int_0^1 f_1(x)\,dx = \varepsilon$, so that $|S(f_1) - g| \le \varepsilon$, i.e., the NO answer produced by our algorithm is wrong. In short, we see that no algorithm can give correct answers to the verification problem for this integration example. □

Since we generally cannot solve verification in the worst case setting, we must either use a different setting or redefine the task if we want to verify proposed solutions. We briefly examine each approach.

We first consider the *probabilistic setting*. This requires a probability measure μ on the class F of problem elements. Verification for the probabilistic setting is defined as follows. Let

$$\text{Fail}(U) = \sup_{g \in G} \mu\{\, f \in F : U(f, g) \neq \text{VER}(f, g)\,\},$$

be the probabilistic failure of an approximation U to the verification operator, i.e., the measure of the largest set for which $U(\cdot, g)$ differs from $\text{VER}(\cdot, g)$. The cost of this approximation is given as

$$\text{cost}^{\text{prob}-\text{ver}}(U) = \sup_{f \in F, g \in G} \text{cost}(U, f, g),$$

where $\text{cost}(U, f, g)$ is the informational cost of computing $y = N(f; g)$ plus the combinatory cost of computing $\phi(y, g)$. Then we are interested in

$$\text{comp}^{\text{prob}-\text{ver}}(\varepsilon, \delta) = \inf\{\, \text{cost}^{\text{prob}-\text{ver}}(U) : U \text{ such that Fail}(U) \leq \delta\,\},$$

the (ε, δ)-probabilistic complexity of the verification problem. Note that we have introduced an additional parameter δ. We are willing to accept an ε-approximation that fails on a set of measure at most δ.

Suppose that

- F is a separable Banach space,
- μ is a Gaussian measure with zero mean,
- S is a continuous linear functional,
- Λ, the set of permissible information operations, is a subset of F^*, the continuous linear functionals on F. For example, if F is a function space that is embedded in a space of continuous functions, then standard information qualifies.

As we will see, verification can be either trivial or exponentially harder than computation, depending on the relation between ε and δ. Let

$$\sigma_0 = \int_F |S(f)|^2\, \mu(df)$$

denote the variance of the a posteriori measure μS^{-1} on the solution elements. Woźniakowski [1992c] considered two cases. First, suppose that

$$\sqrt{\frac{2}{\pi}} \int_0^{\varepsilon/\sqrt{\sigma_0}} e^{-t^2/2}\, dt \leq \delta. \tag{11.2}$$

Then the failure set of the approximation $U \equiv \text{NO}$ has measure at most δ. Hence the trivial "NO" algorithm is optimal, and so $\text{comp}^{\text{prob}-\text{ver}}(\varepsilon, \delta) =$

0 whenever (11.2) holds. On the other hand, suppose that (11.2) does not hold. Then the (ε, δ)-complexity of verification is related to the probabilistic complexity of *computation* in the probabilistic setting, which is defined by taking

$$\operatorname{card}(N) \equiv \operatorname{card}^{\mathrm{prob-com}}(N) := \sup_{f \in F} n(f),$$

$$e(U, \delta) \equiv e^{\mathrm{prob-com}}(U, \delta) := \inf_{A:\mu(A) \leq \delta} \sup_{f \in F - A} \|S(f) - U(f)\|,$$

$$\operatorname{cost}(U) \equiv \operatorname{cost}^{\mathrm{prob-com}}(U) := \sup_{f \in F} \operatorname{cost}(U(f)),$$

$$\operatorname{comp}(\varepsilon, \delta) \equiv \operatorname{comp}^{\mathrm{prob-com}}(\varepsilon, \delta)$$
$$:= \inf\{\operatorname{cost}(U) : U \text{ such that } e^{\mathrm{prob-com}}(U, \delta) \leq \varepsilon\}.$$

We have

$$\operatorname{comp}^{\mathrm{prob-ver}}(\varepsilon, \delta) \sim \operatorname{comp}^{\mathrm{prob-com}}(\varepsilon, e^{-(a\varepsilon/\delta)^2}),$$

where $a = a^*/(2\pi\sqrt{\sigma_0})$ for some $a^* \in [1, 2]$. Moreover, adaptive information is no better than nonadaptive information. Hence verification is exponentially harder than computation.

For further discussion of verification, as well as optimal algorithms for the probabilistic setting, see Woźniakowski [1992c].

Next, we consider *relaxed verification* in the worst case setting. Novak & Woźniakowski [1992] studied relaxed verification, introducing an additional relaxation parameter $\alpha > 0$, and redefining the verification operator as

$$\operatorname{VER}(f, g) = \begin{cases} \text{YES} & \text{if } \|S(f) - g\| \leq \varepsilon, \\ \text{NO} & \text{if } \|S(f) - g\| > (1 + \alpha)\varepsilon, \\ \text{YES or NO} & \text{otherwise.} \end{cases}$$

That is, we want to verify whether the elements $S(f)$ and g differ in norm by at most ε, differ by at least $(1 + \alpha)\varepsilon$, or lie in the safety zone between these bounds.

Novak & Woźniakowski [1992] studied connections between the worst case complexities $\operatorname{comp}^{\mathrm{ver}}(\cdot, \cdot)$ and $\operatorname{comp}^{\mathrm{com}}(\cdot)$ of relaxed verification and computation. They established that

$$\operatorname{comp}^{\mathrm{ver}}(\varepsilon, \alpha) \leq \operatorname{comp}^{\mathrm{com}}(\varepsilon\alpha/2) + 1$$

for any problem, linear or nonlinear. This bound is essentially sharp, since

$$\operatorname{comp}^{\mathrm{ver}}(\varepsilon, \alpha) \sim \operatorname{comp}^{\mathrm{com}}(\varepsilon\alpha/2)$$

when S is a linear functional.

What can we say when S is not a linear functional? Suppose that adaption does not help for relaxed verification. Then

$$\text{comp}^{\text{ver}}(\varepsilon, \alpha) \geq \text{comp}^{\text{com}}(\eta),$$

where $\eta = \Theta(\varepsilon\alpha)$, and thus

$$\text{comp}^{\text{ver}}(\varepsilon, \alpha) \sim \text{comp}^{\text{com}}\big(\Theta(\varepsilon\alpha)\big).$$

On the other hand, they showed that if S is a linear diagonal operator on ℓ_p, then

$$\text{comp}^{\text{ver}}(\varepsilon, \alpha) = \Theta\big(\text{comp}^{\text{com}}(\varepsilon\alpha^r)\big),$$

for small α, where

$$r = \begin{cases} 1/p & \text{if } p \in [1, 2], \\ 1/2 & \text{if } p \in [2, \infty), \\ 1 & \text{if } p = \infty. \end{cases}$$

This means that adaption helps significantly for the relaxed problem when $p > 1$.

12

Complexity of Implementation Testing

Lee & Woźniakowski [1995a] studied implementation testing for continuous problems. They described their motivation as follows:

With advanced computer technology, large systems are often built to fulfill complicated tasks. As the systems get larger, they become less reliable. Testing has become an indispensable part of system design and analysis; however, it has proved to be a formidable task for complex systems. Testing may have a variety of forms in different areas of science and technology. ... The task is: we have a specification of a system design and we want to test if a given implementation conforms to the specification based on the observed system input and output behavior. ... For finite state system testing, research was initiated in the 50's by Moore [1956]. It has drawn much attention both from theoretical computer science and system research due to its applications to sequential circuit testing (Friedman & Menon [1971]), which started in the early 60's, and to communication protocol testing in recent years. ... Moore [1956] first showed that with a finite number of tests it can be checked if an implementation machine conforms to the specification machine; such a test sequence is called a checking experiment. Hennie [1964] provided an elegant algorithm for constructing a checking experiment of exponential length. Recently, polynomial time algorithms were obtained, see Lee & Yannakakis [1995], and the problem of state identification and verification was also resolved, see Lee & Yannakakis [1994].

However, as we have observed a number of times in this book, scientific and engineering problems are often modeled by continuous mathematical formulations. For continuous problems, there are *infinitely* many inputs. Since we will charge for each test, we can permit only a *finite* number of tests. It is not at all clear that implementation testing of continuous problems can be achieved with only a finite number of tests and, indeed, the worst case results are negative. Can we get positive results by weakening the assurance?

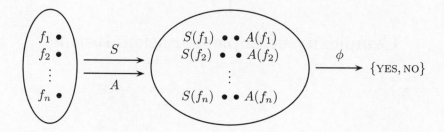

Fig. 12.1 Implementation testing

By introducing operators into the formalization of implementation testing, Lee and Woźniakowski were able to use IBC tools to attack this problem. Assume that we are given a *specification* operator $S\colon F \to G$ and an implementation operator $A\colon F \to G$. It is assumed that we know the input/output behavior of both S and A, i.e., that for any $f \in F$, we can obtain both $S(f)$ and $A(f)$. We perform a finite number of tests on elements $f_1, \ldots, f_n$, and we wish to determine whether A "conforms to" S, on the basis of the test results.

Implementation testing is represented by Figure 12.1; this may be compared with Figures 2.2 and 11.1, which represent computation and verification, respectively.

We will focus on linear testing, i.e., both the specification operator S and the implementation operator A are linear.

Remark: It might appear natural to assume that whenever the specification operator is linear, then the implementation operator should also be linear. However, this assumption is actually quite restrictive, since the implementation operator will generally be nonlinear, e.g., when adaptive sampling and termination criteria are used.   □

Suppose first that F is of finite dimension n. In that case, we can test on a basis $\{f_1, \ldots, f_n\}$. We see that $A \equiv S$ (i.e., the implementation is correct) iff $A(f_i) = S(f_i)$ for $1 \le i \le n$. However, if F is of infinite dimension, then a finite number of tests will never suffice to guarantee correctness. Indeed, no matter how we choose $f_1, \ldots, f_n$, there exist a linear operator A and an element f_{n+1} such that $A(f_i) = S(f_i)$ for $1 \le i \le n$, but $A(f_{n+1}) \ne S(f_{n+1})$.

Of course, this result is not as pessimistic as it appears, since we typically do not expect exact answers for numerical computations. So we instead wish to conclude that

$$\sup_{f \in F} \|S(f) - A(f)\| \le \varepsilon \qquad (12.1)$$

(in the worst case setting) or that

$$\left(\int_F \|S(f) - A(f)\|^2 \, \mu(df) \right)^{1/2} \le \varepsilon \qquad (12.2)$$

(in the average case setting), after a finite number of tests. An implementation A that satisfies the appropriate bound (12.1) or (12.2) *conforms* to the specification S; otherwise, it *fails*.

Clearly, the choice of F must play a role here. To be specific, we shall only consider the case where F is a subset of some Hilbert space H. For the worst case setting, we shall choose F to be an ellipsoid in H, while in the average case setting, we let $F = H$.

We add one final requirement. Any faulty implementation A is likely to be detected if it differs drastically from the specification S. It is therefore reasonable to assume that we know an a priori upper bound $\|S - A\| \le K$.

Under these hypotheses, Lee & Woźniakowski [1995a] proved that finite testing is inconclusive, in both the worst case and average case settings.

Thus if we want to solve the testing problem, we must weaken the assurance. One idea is to settle for testing in the limit. Choose an infinite test sequence $f_1, f_2, \ldots$. We test each f_i, obtaining $A(f_i)$ and $S(f_i)$, and guessing

$$d_i = \begin{cases} \text{YES} & \text{if we believe } A \text{ conforms to } S, \\ \text{NO} & \text{otherwise.} \end{cases}$$

Suppose now that we are given an implementation A and a specification S, such that $S - A$ is continuous. (That is, we no longer require a known a priori bound on $\|S - A\|$.) Lee & Woźniakowski [1995a] designed a test sequence $\{f_i\}_{i=1}^\infty$, as well as a corresponding decision sequence $\{d_i\}_{i=1}^\infty$, such that only finitely many of the d_i are wrong. More precisely, for any $f \in F$, there exists a finite integer $n(f)$ such that the guesses d_i are correct for all $i \ge n(f)$.

Moreover the test sequence $\{f_i\}_{i=1}^\infty$ is *universal*, in the sense that it depends on the parameters ε and α, as well as the ellipsoid F, but it is independent of the specification operator S and the implementation operator A. This means that we can determine the test sequence once and for all, independent of which specification operator we are trying to emulate and which implementation operator we are trying to use for the emulation. Furthermore, this test sequence consists of orthogonal elements on the boundary of the ellipsoid F, which gives a theoretical basis supporting the conventional wisdom of using boundary cases as test values when doing numerical testing.

Unfortunately, this result is primarily of theoretical interest, since $n(f)$ can be arbitrarily large. So we turn to another idea. Recall the results in Chapter 11, where we mentioned that whereas the verification problem is unsolvable, relaxed verification is solvable. Perhaps we can solve a relaxed form of the testing problem.

To this end, we will introduce a relaxation parameter α. We shall say that an implementation A *weakly conforms* to S if

$$\sup_{f \in F} \|S(f) - A(f)\| \leq \varepsilon(1 + \alpha),$$

and (as before) is *faulty* if

$$\sup_{f \in F} \|S(f) - A(f)\| > \varepsilon.$$

Just as with the verification problem, there is a safety zone, i.e., we may have

$$\varepsilon < \sup_{f \in F} \|S(f) - A(f)\| \leq \varepsilon(1 + \alpha).$$

We summarize results about relaxed testing for both the worst case setting and the average case setting. The worst case setting was studied in Lee & Woźniakowski [1995a], where the following results were established:

(i) The relaxed testing problem is solvable in the worst case setting.

(ii) There exists a universal test set for relaxed testing; it consists of orthogonal elements on the boundary of F.

(iii) The minimal number of tests required for the relaxed testing problem is close to the number of tests used by the universal test set described in (ii) above. Hence, the universal test set is essentially optimal.

The average case setting was studied in Lee & Woźniakowski [1997]; the main results are:

(i) A finite number of tests from an arbitrary complete orthogonal basis is conclusive.

(ii) The eigenvectors of the covariance operator of the probability measure yield an almost optimal test sequence. This sequence is universal.

Having discussed the linear testing problem, we now turn to the non-linear testing problem, studied in Lee & Woźniakowski [1995b]. Once again, finite testing is inconclusive. They find that testing nonlinear operators is again decidable in the limit. Since the number $n(f)$ of tests can be arbitrarily large, they consider relaxed testing. Whereas a finite test set is once again conclusive for relaxed testing, the cost may be prohibitive. To surmount these difficulties, the authors consider probabilistic variants of the testing problems. They say that an implementation β-*conforms* to the specification if the measure of the failure set is at most β; it β-*fails* otherwise. Lee & Woźniakowski [1995b] present a simple probabilistic algorithm, based on random sampling in F, which determines β-conformance or β-failure. However, random sampling in an infinite-dimensional space is prohibitively expensive, if not impossible. Fortunately, for weak β-conformance testing, it suffices to draw random samples from finite-dimensional subspaces of F. Finally, the test sequences for testing nonlinear operators are all universal, being provided by an ε-net of the input set.

We close this chapter by briefly comparing the "three legs" of IBC—computation, verification, and implementation testing—which are represented in Figures 2.2, 11.1, and 12.1:

(i) The computation problem is to compute an ε-approximation to $S(f)$.

(ii) The verification problem is to verify whether a given element g is within a distance ε of the solution element $S(f)$. This is a decision problem.

(iii) The implementation testing problem is to determine whether a given implementation A computes an ε-approximation to a specification operator S. This is a decision problem.

Note that for all three cases, we have only partial information about problem elements f.

13

Noisy Information

We have previously mentioned that information-based complexity is the branch of computational complexity that deals with problems for which the information is partial, noisy, and priced. Up to this point, we have ignored the effects of noise, concentrating on exact partial information. But much of the information available in practice will be noisy, the sources of contamination including

- measurement errors,
- rounding errors, and
- deliberate falsification by an adversary.

The study of noisy information has lagged due, at least in part, to the technical difficulties. One important early paper is Micchelli & Rivlin [1977] in which they obtained some general results for information with bounded noise. There has been much recent progress. See Plaskota [1996c], an authoritative monograph on what's been accomplished, as well as much new material.

We provide an example of noisy information.

Example: The integration problem: Consider the integration problem of Chapter 2:

$$F = \{\, [0,1] \xrightarrow{f} \mathbb{R} : \mathrm{Lip}(f) \leq 1 \,\},$$
$$S(f) = \int_0^1 f(x)\,dx \qquad \forall f \in F,$$
$$N(f) = [f(t_1), \ldots, f(t_n)] \qquad \forall f \in F.$$

This is a problem for which we have exact partial information. Suppose now that instead of observing $N(f)$, we can only observe

$$y = [y_1, \ldots, y_n]$$

where

$$y_i = f(t_i) + \xi_i \qquad (1 \leq i \leq n).$$

The information is noisy.

We consider two kinds of noisy information, each leading to a different way of defining worst case error. If we know that $\|\xi\| \leq \delta$ for some norm $\| \cdot \|$ on $\mathbb{R}^n$, then the problem has *bounded noise*. The error of an algorithm ϕ is defined as

$$e^{\text{wor}-\text{wor}}(\phi, N) = \sup_{f \in F} \sup_{\substack{y \in \mathbb{R}^n \\ \|y - N(f)\| \leq \delta}} |S(f) - \phi(y)|.$$

We are combining a worst case over problem elements with worst case over noisy information.

Alternatively, if we know that the noise ξ is given by a probability distribution π, then the problem has *stochastic noise*. (For example, we might know that the ξ_is are independent random variables, normally distributed with mean zero and variance σ^2.) Then the worst case error of an algorithm ϕ for the case of stochastic noise is defined as

$$e^{\text{wor}-\text{avg}}(\phi, N) = \sup_{f \in F} \left(\int_{\mathbb{R}^n} |S(f) - \phi(N(f) + \xi)|^2 \, \pi(d\xi) \right)^{1/2}. \qquad (13.1)$$

Note that this setting combines the worst case over problem elements with the average case over noisy information.† $\qquad\qquad\qquad\square$

Remark: Up to this point, this book has been concerned with problems for which we have only partial information. However, once we allow inexact information, information-level arguments can be used for problems with complete, yet noisy, information. Applications include many problems of estimation and control, arising in areas such as system identification, parameter and state estimation, and prediction. Information-based techniques have been successfully used to solve such problems, see Bai *et al.* ([1995], [1996], [1997], [1998]), Kacewicz & Milanese [1995], Milanese & Belforte [1982], Milanese & Kacewicz [1994], Milanese & Tempo [1985], Milanese *et al.* [1986], and Vicino *et al.* [1987]. $\qquad\square$

Example: The integration problem (continued): Consider bounded noise in the ℓ_∞-norm, so that

$$|y_i - f(t_i)| \leq \delta \qquad (1 \leq i \leq n).$$

---

† We could also consider noisy information for the average case setting, giving "average-average" and "average-worst" settings for noisy information.

The nth minimal error is

$$\frac{1}{4n} + \delta,$$

the optimal evaluation points are

$$t_i^* = \frac{2i-1}{2n} \qquad (1 \le i \le n),$$

and the optimal algorithm is

$$\phi(y) = \int_0^1 p(y;t)\,dt,$$

where $p(y;\cdot)$ is the natural spline of degree 1 that interpolates the noisy data $y = [y_1, \ldots, y_n]$. For further discussion, see p. 84 of Plaskota [1996c]. □

Although a full discussion is beyond the scope of this monograph, we next mention a surprising result of Plaskota [1996b], namely, that in some sense, noisy information is sometimes better than exact information!

Example: Let $d \ge 2$, and consider the integration problem given by

$$F = \{\, [0,1]^d \xrightarrow{f} \mathbb{R} : \mathrm{Lip}(f) \le 1 \,\},$$

$$S(f) = \int_{[0,1]^d} f(x)\,dx \qquad \forall f \in F,$$

$$N(f) = [f(t_1), \ldots, f(t_n)] \qquad \forall f \in F.$$

For $f \in F$, assume that we have information

$$y = N(f) + \xi$$

with stochastic noise ξ, where $\xi_1, \ldots, \xi_n$ are independent random variables, normally distributed with a mean of zero and a variance of σ^2. We let $r^{\mathrm{non}}(n, \sigma)$ and $r^{\mathrm{a}}(n, \sigma)$ respectively denote the nonadaptive and adaptive nth minimal radii for this problem. Suppose first that $\sigma = 0$, i.e., we have no noise. Then the integral in (13.1) disappears, and we have the usual worst case setting, so that

$$r^{\mathrm{non}}(n, 0) = r^{\mathrm{a}}(n, 0) = \Theta(n^{-1/d}).$$

On the other hand, if $\sigma > 0$, we have

$$r^{\mathrm{non}}(n, \sigma) = \Theta(n^{-1/d}),$$

while

$$r^{\mathrm{a}}(n,\sigma) = \Theta(n^{-1/2}).$$

Here, the Θ-factors are independent of d. The nth minimal error algorithm (using adaptive information) is the arithmetic mean of n noisy function evaluations; the optimal sample points depend explicitly on σ.

□

What does this result tell us? For exact information, the results for nonadaptive and adaptive information are the same. Moreover, we suffer from the curse of dimensionality. However, there is a radical change when we consider noisy information. For nonadaptive information, we still suffer from the curse of dimensionality. But if we allow adaption, the curse is dispelled, since the number of function evaluations is independent of the dimension d. This means that if

- we are trying to solve the integration problem for large d,
- we are willing to live with the weakened assurance provided by (13.1), and
- the distribution of the noise is known,

then noisy information is better than exact information.

As our final example of noisy information, we discuss clock synchronization in distributed networks. In the mid-1980s, there was a series of papers on this problem; see, for example, Halpern *et al.* [1985] and Lynch & Lundelius [1985]. In these papers, the transmission times (for short delays) were assumed to be deterministic, and the performance of algorithms was measured by the worst case with respect to delays. The following negative result is due to Lynch & Lundelius [1985]: Even for a completely connected network with k processors and with delays taking any values between L and H, no algorithm can synchronize the clocks better than $\delta = (H - L)(k - 1)/k$, no matter how many messages are sent. Since $\frac{1}{2}(H - L) \le \delta < H - L$, it is impossible to synchronize the clocks if $H - L$ is large.

Halpern *et al.* [1985] wrote

In practice, of course, message transmission times are best viewed as being randomly chosen from a probability distribution. ... Finding the best strategy for processors to follow to achieve optimal precision as a function of the probability distribution on message delivery time remains a completely open problem.

This stimulated the work of Wasilkowski [1989a], who made the following assumptions. The network is viewed as a strongly connected undirected graph, with nodes representing processors and edges representing communication links. Each processor P_i has a local nondrifting clock D_i running at a real time rate. Thus $D_i(t) = t + \xi_i$, where ξ_i are unknown. The problem is to find an algorithm which "shifts" the clocks so that the error, i.e., the largest difference between any two shifted clocks, is as small as possible.

To synchronize the clocks, processors communicate by sending local clock readings. Wasilkowski assumed that the time to transmit a message is a random variable with a known probability distribution, say, uniform on the interval $[L, H]$. He defined the average error of an algorithm as the expected difference between any two shifted clocks. Obviously, the more messages sent, the smaller the error. On the other hand, each message costs. Thus there is a trade-off between error and cost. He studied the following two questions:

(i) For a network with k processors and a fixed number n, what is the minimal average error among all algorithms that use n messages?

(ii) What is the algorithm whose average error is minimal?

He called such an algorithm *optimal* and its (average) error, denoted by error(n, k), the nth *minimal error*.

We mention some of Wasilkowski's results, beginning with the simple case of two processors, $k = 2$, and uniformly distributed delays. The nth minimal error equals

$$\text{error}(n, 2) = \frac{H - L}{\sqrt{2(n + 1)(n + 2)}}.$$

The optimal algorithm is simple to implement. Since it uses unidirectional messages, it is free of deadlocks. It uses only n additions and at most $2n - 2$ comparisons and can be implemented so that all messages except one are single-bit messages. Furthermore, this algorithm is robust in the following sense: if n_1 messages are lost, the average error of the algorithm is equal to the $(n - n_1)$th minimal error.

Similar results hold for $k = 2$ with arbitrary symmetric distributions of delays. More precisely, for an arbitrary symmetric distribution, the optimal algorithm uses unidirectional messages, and is equal to the Pitman estimator; see, e.g., Ferguson [1967].

Now assume that the network has k processors and an arbitrary topology. Then for an arbitrary symmetric distribution of delays,

$$\text{error}(n,k) \geq \text{error}\left(\left\lfloor \frac{n}{k-1} \right\rfloor, 2\right).$$

For the uniform distribution,

$$\text{error}(n,k) \geq \frac{(H-L)(k-1)}{\sqrt{2(n+k-1)(n+2k-2)}}.$$

Wasilkowski obtains an almost optimal algorithm ϕ^*. This algorithm is defined in terms of a minimal diameter tree T that spans the network, and its expected error depends on the diameter, $\text{diam}(T)$, of T. The expected error of the algorithm ϕ^* equals

$$\text{error}\left(\left\lfloor \frac{n}{k-1} \right\rfloor, 2\right)\sqrt{\text{diam}(T)}.$$

Thus

$$\text{error}\left(\left\lfloor \frac{n}{k-1} \right\rfloor, 2\right) \leq \text{error}(n,k) \leq \text{error}\left(\left\lfloor \frac{n}{k-1} \right\rfloor, 2\right)\sqrt{\text{diam}(T)}.$$

The gap between the lower bound on $\text{error}(n,k)$ and the error of ϕ^* is at most $\sqrt{\text{diam}(T)} \leq \sqrt{k-1}$. This means that ϕ^* is almost optimal for small k. For certain networks the gap is even smaller. Indeed, for a completely connected network one can choose T with $\sqrt{\text{diam}(T)} = \sqrt{2}$, and for a square array network, one can choose T with $\sqrt{\text{diam}(T)} = \sqrt{2\sqrt{k}-1}$. The algorithm ϕ^* is free of deadlocks and can be implemented so that all but $k-1$ of the messages are single-bit messages.

14

Value of Information in Computation

A new concept for measuring information, called the *value of information*, was introduced by Packel *et al.* [1992]. They compared the value of information with the entropy-based concept of mutual information, as defined in information theory. The two measures were shown to agree in certain cases and differ in others. The authors discussed why they believed that the value of information is superior in the cases where the two measures differ.

Since Packel *et al.* [1992] is rather technical, we use this opportunity to lay out the issues rather informally. It also provides us the opportunity to contrast concepts of IBC with information theory.

The importance of quantifying the concept of information and of measuring its value is evidenced by the variety of scientific disciplines that have made significant contributions to this problem. Fascination with a notion of entropy to represent disorder, uncertainty, or loss of information has been a major theme of scientific thought. The development of entropy may be traced, starting with the work of Clausius and Boltzmann in the nineteenth century, to Shannon's 1948 development of information theory, and to Kolmogorov's 1955 use of entropy as a measure of capacity in abstract metric spaces. (See Packel *et al.* [1992] for further discussion and references.)

The value of information proposed in Packel *et al.* [1992] emerges from ideas in IBC. In considering problems with incomplete information, we are engaged in "information processing" in the following general sense. Starting with an a priori set or a measure on the set of problem elements, we are able to gather a finite amount of data in the form of measurements, computations, etc. (our information). This information yields an a posteriori set or distribution of problem elements and provides a foundation for designing algorithms to (approximately) solve the given problem.

To obtain the value of this information, we use the *radius of information* $r(N)$, which measures the intrinsic uncertainty due to the information N. We reiterate that the radius of information is one of the most basic concepts of IBC. Of course, the radius of information also depends on the solution operator S and the problem elements F, but we explicitly indicate this dependence only when necessary.

Some researchers in information theory have suggested that the standard information-theoretic measures of entropy and mutual information can provide the desired measure of the value of information. The radius of information seems to provide the basis for a natural and more general measure for continuous problems. In particular, the radius of information is always well-defined even for the infinite-dimensional problems often considered in IBC. The radius-based value of information agrees with the mutual information as obtained from the continuous analogue of Shannon entropy in some important cases. In other cases, however, the two measures disagree.

Recall that the radius of information $r^{\text{wor}}(N)$ for the worst case setting was defined on p. 19. The most important property of $r^{\text{wor}}(N)$ is that it measures the *intrinsic uncertainty* of solving a problem with the given information N. Modulo the assumption that infima are attained, an ε-approximation can be computed iff $r^{\text{wor}}(N) \le \varepsilon$.

Although the radius of information can be defined for every setting of IBC, we'll mainly confine ourselves here to $r^{\text{avg}}(N)$, the average case radius of information N, since we want to compare and contrast with entropy-based concepts from information theory.

The average radius of information $r^{\text{avg}}(N)$ was originally defined in Wasilkowski [1983] (see also Section 6.3 of Traub *et al.* [1988] and Packel *et al.* [1992]). This definition is more subtle than that of the worst case radius. Again, $r^{\text{avg}}(N)$ measures the *intrinsic uncertainty* of solving a problem with the given information N, but now with an average case error criterion. Once again modulo the assumption that infima are attained, an average case ε-approximation can be computed iff $r^{\text{avg}}(N) \le \varepsilon$.

Figure 14.1 illustrates (for linear S and Gaussian μ with zero mean, with μS^{-1} one-dimensional) how information obtained during a computation changes what we know about the solution. The curve on the left shows the a priori density given by the measure before any information is gathered, while the curve on the right shows the a posteriori condi-

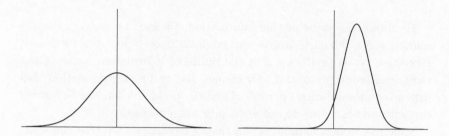

Fig. 14.1 A priori vs. a posteriori density functions

tional density after information N has been computed. The effect of the information is to shift the mean and to reduce the spread of the density.

The uncertainty of the a priori density is measured by $r^{\text{avg}}(0)$, where $N = 0$ means that no information has been obtained. The uncertainty of the a priori conditional density is measured by $r^{\text{avg}}(N)$. Packel *et al.* [1992] defined the *value of information N* for a problem as

$$V(N) = \lg \frac{r^{\text{avg}}(0)}{r^{\text{avg}}(N)},$$

with $\lg = \log_2$ and with $0/0 = \infty/\infty = 1$.

Since the radius of information measures inherent uncertainty, the use of the base 2 logarithm can be interpreted as measuring the number of bits of accuracy provided by the information. By subtracting a "no information" accuracy from the accuracy with information N, we obtain the number of bits of increased accuracy provided by the information N. (Since we are using the average case error criterion, these quantities should be interpreted "on the average.")

We remind the reader of the definitions of entropy and mutual information from information theory, beginning with the discrete case. Given a discrete (atomic) probability space (X, μ), the entropy is defined as

$$H(X) = -\sum_{x \in X} \mu(x) \lg \mu(x).$$

Thus if we have, in addition, a discrete probability space (Y, ν) and a family of conditional probability measures $\nu(\cdot|y)$ over X, the *average mutual information between X and Y* is given by

$$I(X; Y) = H(X) - H(X|Y).$$

The $H(X|Y)$ term is the expected value over Y of the entropies $H(X|y)$ of the conditional probability measures $\nu(\cdot|y)$ on X.

For continuous problems, however, the domain F of problem elements and the range Z of solution elements are generally infinite-dimensional with a priori distributions μ and $\nu = \mu S^{-1}$ that are nonatomic. Even if Z is finite-dimensional and the existence of a continuous density function p for ν is assumed, the "natural" analogue

$$H(X) = - \int_X p(x) \lg p(x)\, dx$$

to the discrete entropy for $X = (Z, \nu)$ is successful in some contexts but problematical in others (see the references in Packel *et al.* [1992] for further discussion). The same problems are inherited by the mutual information in continuous settings.

Nonetheless, there are important cases when the mutual information and the value of information are equal. Packel *et al.* [1992] analyzed two examples. The first was continuous binary search, in which we seek to approximate a real number f from the unit interval with the information gained from asking n "true or false" questions. They assumed that f is uniformly distributed on the unit interval. The second example was integration of continuous functions with the prior chosen as the classical Wiener measure.

They showed that for these two examples, $V(N) = I(X; Y)$. Under what general conditions will the value of information equal the mutual information? Note that in the second example, the problem is to approximate a continuous linear functional. Theorem 2 of Packel *et al.* [1992] provided rather general conditions under which $V(N) = I(X; Y)$ for problems defined by a continuous linear functional.

What if S is not a linear functional? Packel *et al.* [1992] gave a simple example where $S(F)$ has dimension k, with $k \geq 2$. Then $I(X; Y) = +\infty$ while $V(N)$ is well-defined. They also showed that if the relative error criterion is used, then even under the hypotheses of their Theorem 2 (where S is a linear functional), $V(N) \neq I(X; Y)$.

We summarize the desirable properties that $V(N)$ has in measuring the value of information obtained during a computation that involves partial information.

- Although we have focused on the average case in this chapter, the radius of information is defined in all IBC settings and therefore $V(N)$

may be defined in all settings as

$$V(N) = \lg \frac{r(0)}{r(N)}.$$

- $V(N)$ has a natural interpretation in terms of gain in bits of accuracy.
- $V(N)$ agrees with the concept of mutual information $I(X;Y)$ for some computational problems. It sensibly disagrees in a variety of situations. In particular, it avoids the well-known difficulties of defining $I(X;Y)$ for nonatomic probability measures.
- The information-theoretic notion of mutual information and the statistical notion of variance do not depend upon an error criterion, whereas the value of information does.
- The radius $r(N)$ is an intrinsic measure of the uncertainty in the solution if information N is available. Therefore $V(N)$ is also an intrinsic measure.

15

Assigning Values to Mathematical Hypotheses

Traub & Woźniakowski [1991a] suggest that computational complexity permits us to quantify the value of mathematical hypotheses. We give a brief exposition of this idea.

Since complexity is an intrinsic property of a problem, any change in complexity which stems from using hypothesis H_1 rather than hypothesis H_2 is solely due to the change in hypothesis. Computational complexity can be used to see the effect of assuming properties such as convexity and smoothness of functions, or symmetry and positive definiteness of matrices.

Three applications will illustrate this idea:

- integration of smooth scalar functions,
- convexity versus smoothness in nonlinear optimization,
- positive definiteness in large linear systems.

For simplicity, we confine ourselves to the worst case setting.

Integration

The complexity of univariate integration for the unit ball of functions having smoothness r is

$$\text{comp}(\varepsilon) = \Theta\left(\left(\frac{1}{\varepsilon}\right)^{1/r}\right).$$

Thus, for integration, we know the effect of changing the smoothness hypothesis. For example, if we change from once differentiable to twice-differentiable, the complexity decreases by a factor of $1/\sqrt{\varepsilon}$.

Indeed, many problems defined for scalar functions have complexity of order $(1/\varepsilon)^{1/r}$. Examples may be found in Chapter 5 of Traub *et al.* [1988]. In such cases, we know how smoothness affects complexity.

Nonlinear Optimization

Nemirovsky & Yudin [1983] and Nemirovsky & Nesterov [1994] study a rather general nonlinear constrained optimization problem for both smooth and convex functions. Their results tell us how much easier the assumption of convexity makes the problem.

The problem is to minimize a nonlinear function subject to nonlinear constraints. Let $f = [f_0, f_1, \ldots, f_m]$, where f_0 denotes the objective function and $f_1, \ldots, f_m$ denote the constraints. Let F denote a class of functions f defined on a nonempty compact subset D of $\mathbb{R}^d$.

First, let $F = F_r$ be the class of r times continuously differentiable functions such that the rth derivative of f_j in any direction is uniformly bounded. Then

$$\mathrm{comp}_r(\varepsilon) = \Theta\left(\left(\frac{1}{\varepsilon}\right)^{d/r}\right).$$

Thus, the problem is intractable for the class of smooth functions.

Now, let $F = F_c$ be the class of *convex* functions that satisfy a Lipschitz condition with a uniform constant. The complexity for this class of convex functions is of the form

$$\mathrm{comp}_c(\varepsilon) = \Theta\left(\log \frac{1}{\varepsilon}\right),$$

where the constant in the Θ-notation depends polynomially on d and m. Thus, for convex functions, the problem is tractable.

These results quantify the relative value of smoothness and convexity for this optimization problem.

Large Linear Systems

Traub & Woźniakowski [1984] study the optimal solution of large linear systems. Let $Ax = b$ denote a large linear system, where A is an $n \times n$ nonsingular large sparse matrix. If all the elements of A and b are known, then the information is complete and we can, in principle, solve the problem exactly by a direct method. However, if n is large, say of order 10^4, then the time of a direct solution may be prohibitive. Furthermore a direct algorithm may require too much storage.

We can adopt the following strategy. Even if the matrix A is available, we will not use it. We will replace the complete information about A with partial information, and settle for an approximate solution. That is, the problem is to compute x such that $\|Ax - b\| \leq \varepsilon$, provided that $\|b\| = 1$. This is the idea behind iterative methods for solving large linear systems.

What partial information about A is it reasonable to know? For sparse matrices, it is reasonable to use matrix-vector products Av, since they can usually be computed in time and storage proportional to n. When determining cost, we only count the number of matrix-vector products.

Assume then that the information about A and b consists of matrix-vector multiplications,

$$N_k(A, b) = [b, Az_1, \ldots, Az_k],$$

where each z_i may depend on b and on the previously computed vectors $Az_1, \ldots, Az_{i-1}$. To be of interest, $k \ll n$. *Krylov information* is the special choice

$$z_i = \begin{cases} b & \text{if } i = 1, \\ Az_{i-1} & \text{if } i \geq 2. \end{cases}$$

Thus Krylov information is given by

$$N_k(A, b) = [b, Ab, \ldots, A^k b].$$

Many of the standard iterative methods, such as conjugate gradient, Chebyshev, minimal residual, and successive approximation, use Krylov information.

Traub & Woźniakowski [1984] conjectured that if A belongs to a class F of orthogonally invariant matrices, then Krylov information and the minimal residual algorithm are optimal. Chou [1987] established optimality up to a multiplicative factor of at most 2. Optimality was settled by Nemirovsky [1992], who gives complexity formulas for $\text{comp}(\varepsilon, F)$ for several classes of matrices, if information consisting of matrix-vector multiplications is used.

For example, we can give a partial answer to how much easier it is to solve a large linear system $Ax = b$ if A is positive definite. Let F_1 be the class of symmetric positive definite matrices with condition numbers uniformly bounded by M. Class F_2 differs from F_1 by the lack of positive definiteness. Then it follows from the general expressions for $\text{comp}(\varepsilon, F_i)$ that

$$\text{comp}(\varepsilon, F_1) \simeq M^{-1/2} \text{comp}(\varepsilon, F_2)$$

for ε small, M large, and n so large that $n > M \ln(2/\varepsilon)$.

This is only a partial answer; why should we limit ourselves to matrix-vector multiplications? If we permit more general information about A, we might lower the complexity or change our conclusion of what positive definiteness is worth.

Traub & Woźniakowski [1991a] consider two generalizations of information consisting of matrix-vector multiplications. One generalization is inner products between rows of A and an arbitrary column vector v. Such inner product information was studied by Rabin [1972] for the exact solution of linear systems, $\varepsilon = 0$, and for an arbitrary matrix A. A further generalization is information consisting of arbitrary linear functionals on A and b.

Complexity results for these two kinds of information are open problems, see Traub & Woźniakowski [1991a].

16

Open Problems

Because IBC is fairly new and covers a very large domain, it is replete with open questions. Packel & Woźniakowski [1987] posed ten open questions; most remain unsolved. Traub & Woźniakowski [1991a] posed eight other open questions; all remain unsolved. Many of the other papers and books in the bibliography state open questions. We have discussed new research directions with other IBC researchers; we will not attempt to convey these here.

A list of open problems from this monograph is provided for the reader's convenience. This list covers a wide spectrum ranging from very specific problems such as (ii) to the very general problem listed as (vii).

(i) [p. 33] Characterize the problems for which randomization breaks intractability.

(ii) [p. 40] For a given strongly tractable problem,

    (a) What are the best values for the exponent p and the constant K in (3.11)?

    (b) Where are the best sample points for calculating an ε-approximation in d dimensions?

(iii) [p. 51] Regarding QMC methods:

    (a) Which financial problems have integrands belonging to F_γ?

    (b) Provide a *deterministic* construction of a strongly tractable QMC method for F_γ.

    (c) What is the best value of the exponent p in (4.4)?

(iv) [p. 52] Characterize classes of integrands for which QMC is superior to MC.

(v) [p. 56] Regarding path integration:

(a) What is the complexity of path integration of entire functions in the worst case setting? Is the algorithm of Wasilkowski and Woźniakowski essentially optimal?

(b) What is the complexity of path integration of entire functions in the randomized setting?

(vi) [p. 60] Is every (measurable) linear operator computable on the average for Gaussian measures?

(vii) [p. 71] Does Gödel's theorem limit scientific knowledge?

(viii) [p. 71] Do intractability theorems limit scientific knowledge?

(ix) [p. 73] Do non-computability results limit scientific knowledge?

(x) [p. 76] Prove the following conjectures concerning linear programming:

(a) The linear inequalities problem does not have polynomial complexity in the real-number model.

(b) The solution of linear inequalities is strictly harder than linear equalities in all reasonable models of computation.

17

A Brief History of Information-Based Complexity

We identify three stages in the history of IBC.

Stage 1: Specific Problems

In this stage, results are typically stated in terms of optimal error rather than complexity. Even the phrase "computational complexity" was not to be introduced until the mid-1960s.

Sard [1949] studied optimal error algorithms using function evaluations at fixed points for scalar integration. He discussed extensions of his results to the approximation of linear functionals. Independently, Nikolskij [1950] posed the same problem and permitted the evaluation points to be optimally chosen. Kiefer [1953] showed that if function evaluations are used, then Fibonacci search is optimal in searching for the maximum of a unimodal function.

Bakhvalov [1959] studied optimal error algorithms for multivariate integrals. Golomb & Weinberger [1959] studied the approximation of linear functionals. Schoenberg [1964] related splines to optimal quadrature. Smolyak [1965] proved that for any linear functional defined on a balanced set and for any information operator consisting of n linear functionals, there exists a linear optimal error algorithm. Emelyanov & Ilin [1967] obtained tight bounds on the error of algorithms for the solution of Fredholm integral equations of the second kind. Bakhvalov [1971] is a very influential paper, dealing with adaption and providing the first easily accessible statement of Smolyak's lemma (cited above). Early work on multigrid methods, which often lead to reduced combinatory cost, may be found in Fedorenko [1964] and Bakhvalov [1966].

Traub ([1961], [1964]) initiated the study of optimal iterative algorithms for nonlinear equations, emphasizing the central role of information. Woźniakowski [1975] introduced the concept of order of information in an abstract space, which provides a general tool for establishing maximal order theorems. Maximal order results, needed to obtain lower bounds on computational complexity (Traub & Woźniakowski [1976]), were obtained for scalar nonlinear equations. Nemirovsky & Yudin [1976] began the study of the information complexity of optimization, which was continued in Nemirovsky & Yudin [1983]; see also Nemirovsky & Nesterov [1994].

Stage 2: General Abstract Theory—Worst Case Setting

Micchelli & Rivlin [1977] studied optimal error algorithms for linear operators. Linear noisy information is included. A general formulation of IBC, primarily in the worst case deterministic setting, appeared as very long technical reports in 1977 and 1978; these were combined into the research monograph Traub & Woźniakowski [1980], in which computational complexity became central. The monograph has an annotated bibliography of over 300 papers and books that were published up to 1979. At the time, IBC was called "analytic complexity," to distinguish it from algebraic complexity.

In the 1980 monograph, uncertainty was measured by a norm. Many of the results contained there easily extend to the case where uncertainty is measured by a metric. Traub *et al.* [1983] showed how uncertainty can be measured without a norm or metric, which is needed for certain applications.

Stage 3: General Abstract Theory—Many Settings, Applications

Since many of the results in the worst case deterministic setting are negative, there's a strong incentive to study complexity in stochastic settings. The first paper to study the computational complexity of randomization for multivariate integrals was probably Bakhvalov [1959]. As far as we know, the first papers dealing with the average case setting with partial information were Suldin [1959], [1960] which studied integration for continuous functions equipped with the classical Wiener measure. Larkin [1972] studied linear operators utilizing a Gaussian measure. Both Suldin and Larkin *assume* linear algorithms using non-adaptive information.

Novak [1988a] studied deterministic, randomized, and average case

IBC problems. The monograph by Traub *et al.* [1988] builds on the work of many researchers to develop a general abstract theory and applications to the worst case, average case, probabilistic, randomized, and asymptotic settings.

Although IBC is developed as an abstract theory, applications typically involve multivariate problems. These typically suffer the curse of dimensionality in the worst case setting. The question of whether the curse can be broken has led to much recent research, which continues. Woźniakowski [1994b] introduced the concept of *strong* tractability, i.e., complexity that is independent of dimension.

Typically, information is contaminated with error due to computation or measurement. Progress on complexity with noisy information has been slowed by the technical difficulty of this area. The monograph Plaskota [1996c] made major progress.

Recent years have witnessed considerable progress on important applications, including the solution of differential and integral equations, control theory, economics, computer graphics, path integration, and mathematical finance.

The past is prelude; we look forward to seeing some of the open questions answered and entirely new research directions explored.

Part Three

The Literature of IBC

18

A Guide to the Literature

The bibliography includes citations from this volume. It also contains some of the material published during or after 1987. For material published before then, see the annotated bibliography in Traub & Woźniakowski [1980], as well as the bibliographies found in Novak [1988a] and Traub *et al.* [1988].

Additional extensive bibliographies may be found in Frank [1997], Heinrich [1996], Keller [1998], Novak [1996], Plaskota [1996c], Ritter [1996b], Sikorski [1998], and Werschulz [1991].

Bibliography

Abu-Mostafa, Y. S. (ed) [1988]. *Complexity in Information Theory.* New York: Springer-Verlag.

Acworth, P., Broadie, M., & Glasserman, P. [1997]. A comparison of some Monte Carlo techniques for option pricing. *Pages 1–18 of:* Niederreiter, H., Hellekalek, P., Larcher, G., & Zinterhof, P. (eds), *Monte Carlo and Quasi-Monte Carlo Methods '96.* New York: Springer-Verlag.

Adler, R. J. [1981]. *The Geometry of Random Fields.* Wiley Series in Probability and Mathematical Statistics. New York: Wiley.

Aird, T. J. & Rice, J. R. [1977]. Systematic search in high dimensional sets. *SIAM J. Numer. Anal.*, **14**, 296–312.

Allgower, E. & Georg, K. [1980]. Simplicial and continuation methods for approximating fixed points and solutions to systems of equations. *SIAM Rev.*, **22**(1), 28–85.

Allgower, E. & Georg, K. [1990]. *Numerical Continuation Methods: An Introduction.* Series in Computational Mathematics, vol. 13. Berlin: Springer-Verlag.

Amman, H., Kendrick, D., & Rust, J. (eds) [1996]. *Handbook of Computational Economics.* Handbooks in Econom., vol. 13. Amsterdam: Elsevier North-Holland.

Arestov, B. B. [1990]. Best recovery of operators, and related problems. *Proc. Steklov Inst. Math.*, **189**, 3–20.

Arnheim, R. [1971]. *Entropy and Art: An Essay on Order and Disorder.* Berkeley: University of California Press.

Aronszajn, N. [1950]. Theory of reproducing kernels. *Trans. Amer. Math. Soc.*, **68**, 337–404.

Babenko, K. I. [1960]. Approximation by trigonometric polynomials in a certain class of periodic functions of several variables. *Soviet Math. Dokl.*, **1**, 672–675.

Babenko, K. I. [1979]. *Theoretical Background and Constructing Computational Algorithms for Mathematical-Physical Problems.* Moscow: Nauka. (In Russian.)

Bai, E. W., Cho, H., & Tempo, R. [1995]. Membership set estimators: size, optimal inputs, complexity and relations with least squares. *IEEE Trans. Circuits Sys.*, **42**, 266–277.

112

Bai, E. W., Nagpal, K. M., & Tempo, R. [1996]. Bounded error parameter estimation: Noise models, recursive algorithms and H_∞ optimality. *Automatica*, **32**, 985–999.

Bai, E. W., Qiu, L., & Tempo, R. [1998]. Unfalsified weighted least square estimates in set-membership identification. *IEEE Trans. Circuits Sys.* (To appear.)

Bai, E. W., Tempo, R., & Nagpal, K. M. [1997]. Recursive system identification in the presence of noise and model uncertainties. *Sys. Control Lett.*, 57–62.

Bakhvalov, N. S. [1959]. On approximate calculation of integrals. *Vestnik MGU, Ser. Mat. Mekh. Astron. Fiz. Khim.*, **4**, 3–18. (In Russian.)

Bakhvalov, N. S. [1962]. On the rate of convergence of deterministic integration processes within the functional classes $W_p^{(l)}$. *Theoret. Prob. Appl.*, **7**, 227. (In Russian.)

Bakhvalov, N. S. [1966]. On the convergence of a relaxation method under natural constraints on an elliptic operator. *Z. Vycisl. Mat. Mat. Fiz.*, **6**, 861–883. (In Russian.)

Bakhvalov, N. S. [1971]. On the optimality of linear methods for operator approximation in convex classes of functions. *USSR Comp. Math. Math. Phys.*, **11**, 244–249.

Barrow, J. D. [1990]. *Theories of Everything*. Oxford: Oxford University Press.

Bellman, R. E. [1957]. *Dynamic Programming*. Princeton, NJ: Princeton University Press.

Ben-David, S., Chor, B., Goldreich, O., & Luby, M. [1992]. On the theory of average case complexity. *J. Comp. Sys. Sci.*, **44**, 193–219.

Birkhoff, G. D. [1933]. *Aesthetic Measure*. Cambridge: Cambridge University Press.

Blum, L., Cucker, F., Shub, M., & Smale, S. [1998]. *Complexity and Real Computation*. New York: Springer-Verlag.

Blum, L., Shub, M., & Smale, S. [1989]. On a theory of computation and complexity over the real numbers: NP-completeness, recursive functions and universal machines. *Bull. Amer. Math. Soc. (New Ser.)*, **21**, 1–46.

Bojanov, B. & Woźniakowski, H. (eds) [1992]. *Optimal Recovery*. New York: Nova Science. (Proceedings of the Second International Symposium on Optimal Algorithms, Varna, May 29–June 2, 1989.)

Boult, T. E. & Sikorski, K. [1987]. Can we approximate zeros of functions with nonzero topological degree? *J. Complexity*, **4**, 317–329.

Boult, T. E. & Sikorski, K. [1989a]. Complexity of computing topological degree of Lipschitz functions in two dimensions. *SIAM J. Sci. Statist. Comp.*, **10**(4), 686–698.

Boult, T. E. & Sikorski, K. [1989b]. An optimal complexity algorithm for computing the topological degree in two dimensions. *SIAM J. Sci. Statist. Comp.*, **10**(4), 686–698.

Boyle, P. P. [1977]. Options: A Monte Carlo approach. *J. Financial Econom.*, **4**, 323–338.

Brass, H. [1988a]. Fast-optimale Formeln zur harmonischen Analyse. *Z. Angew. Math. Mech.*, **68**, T484–T485.

Brass, H. [1988b]. Universal quadrature rules in the space of periodic functions. *Pages 16–24 of: Numerical Integration III*. Intern. Ser. Numer. Math., vol. 85. Basel: Birkhäuser.

Brass, H. [1990]. Optimal estimation rules for functions of high smoothness. *IMA J. Numer. Anal.*, **10**, 129–136.

Brass, H. [1991]. Practical Fourier analysis; error bounds and complexity. *Z. Angew. Math. Mech.*, **71**, 3–20.

Brass, H. [1995]. Zur Konstruktion fast-optimaler Algorithmen in der Numerik. *Abh. Braunschw. Wiss. Ges.*, **46**, 71–78.

Brass, H. [1996]. On the quality of algorithms based on spline interpolation. *Numer. Algorithms*, **13**, 159–177.

Bratley, P., Fox, B. L., & Niederreiter, H. [1992]. Implementation and tests of low-discrepancy sequences. *ACM Trans. Model. Comp. Simul.*, **2**, 195–213.

Brent, R. P., Winograd, S., & Wolfe, P. [1973]. Optimal iterative processes for root finding. *Numer. Math.*, **20**, 327–341.

Bykovskij, V. A. [1985]. *On exact order of optimal quadrature formulas for spaces of functions with bounded mixed derivatives.* Tech. rept. Dalnevostochnoi Center of Academy of Sciences, Vladivostok, USSR. (In Russian.)

Caflisch, R. E., Morokoff, W. J., & Owen, A. B. [1997]. Valuation of mortgage backed securities using Brownian bridges to reduce effective dimension. *J. Comp. Finance*, **1**(1), 27–46.

Calude, C. S., Casti, J., & Dinneen, M. J. [1998]. *Unconventional Models of Computation.* Singapore: Springer-Verlag.

Calvin, J. M. [1997]. Average performance of adaptive algorithms for global optimization. *Ann. Appl. Prob.*, **34**, 711–730.

Chaitin, G. J. [1988]. *Algorithmic Information Theory.* Cambridge Tracts in Theoretical Computer Science. Cambridge: Cambridge University Press.

Chen, H. L., Li, C., & Micchelli, C. A. [1993]. Optimal recovery for some classes of functions with L^2 bounded fractional derivatives. *Pages 141–150 of:* Agarwal, R. P. (ed), *Contributions in Numerical Mathematics (in Memory of L. Collatz)*, vol. 22. Singapore: World Scientific.

Cheng, F., Wasilkowski, G. W., Wang, J., Zhang, C., & Wang, W. [1995]. Parallel B-spline surface interpolation on a mesh-connected processor array. *J. Parallel Distrib. Comp.*, **24**, 224–229.

Chernousko, F. L. [1968]. An optimal algorithm for finding the roots of an approximately computed function. *USSR Comp. Math. Math. Phys.*, **8**, 1–24.

Chorin, A. J. [1973]. Accurate evaluation of Wiener integrals. *Math. Comp.*, **27**, 1–15.

Chou, A. W. [1987]. On the optimality of Krylov information. *J. Complexity*, 26–40.

Chow, C. S. & Tsitsiklis, J. N. [1989]. The complexity of dynamic programming. *J. Complexity*, **5**, 466–488.

Chow, C. S. & Tsitsiklis, J. N. [1991]. An optimal multigrid algorithm for continuous state discrete time stochastic control. *IEEE Trans. Auto. Control*, **36-8**, 898–914.

Chu, M. [1994]. There exists a problem whose computational complexity is any given function of the information complexity. *J. Complexity*, **10**, 445–450.

Cipra, B. [1996]. *What's Happening in the Mathematical Sciences (1995–1996).* Providence, RI: Amer. Math. Soc.

Diaconis, P. [1988]. Bayesian numerical analysis. *Pages 163–175 of:* Gupta, S. S. & Berger, J. O. (eds), *Statistical Decision Theory and Related Topics IV*, vol. 1. New York: Springer-Verlag.

Donoho, D. L. [1994]. Statistical estimation and optimal recovery. *Ann. Statist.*, **22**, 238–270.

Donoho, D. L. & Johnstone, I. M. [1994]. Minimax risk over l_p-balls for l_q-error. *Probab. Theory Related Fields*, **99**, 277–303.

Drmota, M. & Tichy, R. F. [1997]. *Sequences, Discrepancies and Applications*. Lecture Notes in Mathematics, vol. 1651. New York: Springer-Verlag.

Edmonds, J. [1967]. Systems of distinct representatives and linear algebra. *J. Res. Nat. Bur. Standards*, **71B**, 241–245.

Emelyanov, K. V. & Ilin, A. M. [1967]. Number of arithmetic operations necessary for the approximate solution of Fredholm integral equations. *USSR Comp. Math. Math. Phys.*, **7**(4), 259–267.

Fabozzi, F. J. [1992]. *Handbook of Mortgage Backed Securities*. Chicago: Probus Publishing Company.

Fang, K. T. & Wang, Y. [1994]. *Number Theoretic Methods in Statistics*. New York: Chapman and Hall.

Fedorenko, R. P. [1964]. The speed of convergence of one iterative process. *Z. Vycisl. Mat. Mat. Fiz.*, **4**, 559–563. Also in *USSR Comp. Math. Math. Phys.*, **4** [1964]. pp. 227–235.

Ferguson, T. S. [1967]. *Mathematical Statistics: A Decision Theoretic Approach*. New York: Academic Press.

Frank, K. [1997]. *Optimal Numerical Solution of Multivariate Integral Equations*. Aachen: Shaker.

Frank, K. & Heinrich, S. [1994]. Complexity of local solution of integral equations. Schock, E. (ed), *Beiträge zur Angewandten Analysis und Informatik*. Aachen: Shaker.

Frank, K. & Heinrich, S. [1996]. Computing discrepancies of Smolyak quadrature rules. *J. Complexity*, **12**, 287–314.

Frank, K., Heinrich, S., & Pereverzev, S. V. [1996]. Information complexity of multivariate Fredholm integral equations in Sobolev classes. *J. Complexity*, **12**, 17–34.

Friedman, A. D. & Menon, P. R. [1971]. *Fault Detection in Digital Circuits*. Englewood Cliffs, NJ: Prentice-Hall.

Friedman, E. J. & Oren, S. S. [1995]. The complexity of resource allocation and price mechanisms under bounded rationality. *Econom. Theory*, **5**, 225–250.

Gal, S. & Micchelli, C. A. [1980]. Optimal sequential and non-sequential procedures for evaluating a functional. *Appl. Anal.*, **10**, 105–120.

Gao, F. & Wasilkowski, G. W. [1993]. On detecting regularity of functions: a probabilistic analysis. *J. Complexity*, **9**, 373–386.

Garey, M. R. & Johnson, D. S. [1979]. *Computers and Intractability*. San Francisco: Freeman.

Geroch, R. & Hartle, J. B. [1986]. Computability and physical theories. *Found. Phys.*, **6**, 533–550.

Geweke, J. [1996]. Monte Carlo simulation and numerical integration. *Pages 731–800 of:* Amman, H., Kendrick, D., & Rust, J. (eds), *Handbook of Computational Economics*. Handbooks in Econom., vol. 13. Amsterdam: Elsevier North-Holland.

Giarré, L., Milanese, M., & Kacewicz, B. Z. [1997]. Model quality evaluation in set membership identification. *Automatica*, **33**(6), 1133–1140.

Gödel, K. [1931]. Über formal unentscheidbare Sätze der Principia Mathematica und verwandter Systeme 1. *Monatshefte Math. Phys.*, **48**, 173–198.

Golomb, M. & Weinberger, H. F. [1959]. Optimal approximation and error bounds. *Pages 117–190 of:* Langer, R. E. (ed), *On Numerical Approximation.* Madison: Univ. of Wisconsin Press.

Golubev, G. K. & Nussbaum, M. [1990]. A risk bound in Sobolev class regression. *Ann. of Statist.*, **18**, 758–778.

Graf, S., Novak, E., & Papageorgiou, A. F. [1989]. Bisection is not optimal on the average. *Numer. Math.*, **55**, 481–491.

Hadamard, J. [1902]. Sur les problèmes aux dérivées partielles et leur signification physique. *Princeton Univ. Bull.*, **13**, 49–52.

Hadamard, J. [1952]. *Lectures on the Cauchy Problem in Linear Partial Differential Equations.* New York: Dover.

Hald, O. H. [1987]. Approximation of Wiener integrals. *J. Comp. Phys.*, **69**, 460–470.

Halpern, J. Y., Megiddo, N., & Munshi, A. A. [1985]. Optimal precision in the presence of uncertainty. *J. Complexity*, **1**(2), 170–196.

Halton, J. H. [1980]. On the efficiency of certain quasi-random sequences of points in evaluating mult-dimensional integrals. *Numer. Math.*, **2**, 84–90. (Correction: id., 196).

Hammersley, J. M. [1960]. Monte Carlo methods for solving multiple problems. *Ann. New York Acad. Sci.*, **86**, 844–874.

Hammersley, J. M. & Handscomb, D. C. [1964]. *Monte Carlo Methods.* London: Chapman and Hall.

Hammersley, J. M. & Mauldon, J. G. [1956]. General principles of antithetic variates. *Proc. Cambridge Philos. Soc.*, **52**, 476–481.

Hammersley, J. M. & Morton, K. W. [1956]. A new Monte Carlo technique: Antithetic Variates. *Proc. Cambridge Philos. Soc.*, **52**, 449–475.

Haussler, D. [1988]. Quantifying inductive bias: AI learning algorithms and Valiant's learning framework. *Artificial Intelligence*, **36**, 177–221.

Heinrich, S. [1992]. Lower bounds for the complexity of Monte Carlo function approximation. *J. Complexity*, **8**, 277–300.

Heinrich, S. [1993]. Complexity of integral equations and relations to s-numbers. *J. Complexity*, **9**, 141–153.

Heinrich, S. [1994]. Random approximation in numerical analysis. *Pages 123–171 of:* Bierstedt, K. D., Pietsch, A., Ruess, W. M., & Vogt, D. (eds), *Functional Analysis.* New York: Marcel Dekker.

Heinrich, S. [1995]. Variance reduction for Monte Carlo methods by means of deterministic numerical computation. *Monte Carlo Methods Appl.*, **1**, 251–277.

Heinrich, S. [1996]. Complexity theory of Monte Carlo algorithms. *Pages 405–419 of:* Renegar, J., Shub, M., & Smale, S. (eds), *The Mathematics of Numerical Analysis.* Lectures in Applied Mathematics, vol. 32. Providence, RI: Amer. Math. Soc.

Heinrich, S. & Kern, J.-D. [1991]. Parallel information-based complexity. *J. Complexity*, **7**, 339–370.

Heinrich, S. & Mathé, P. [1993]. The Monte Carlo complexity of Fredholm integral equations. *Math. Comp.*, **60**(201), 257–278.

Hennie, F. C. [1964]. Fault detecting experiments for sequential circuits. *Pages 95–110 of: Proceedings of Fifth Annual Symposium on Switching Circuit Theory and Logical Design.*

Hickernell, F. J. [1996]. The mean square discrepancy of randomized nets. *ACM Trans. Model. Comp. Simul.*, **6**, 274–296.

Hickernell, F. J. [1997]. A generalized discrepancy and quadrature error bound. *Math. Comput.*, **66**, 299–322.

Hirsch, M. D., Papadimitriou, C. H., & Vavasis, S. A. [1989]. Exponential lower bounds for finding Brouwer fixed points. *J. Complexity*, **4**, 379–416.

Hofmann, N. & Mathé, P. [1997]. On quasi–Monte Carlo simulation of stochastic differential equations. *Math. Comp.*, **66**(218), 573–589.

Holladay, J. C. [1957]. Smoothest curve approximation. *Math. Tables Aids Comput.*, **11**, 233–243.

Hurwicz, L. [1986]. On informational decentralization and efficiency in resource allocation mechanisms. *Pages 238–350 of:* Reiter, S. (ed), *Studies in Mathematical Economics.* Providence, RI: Math. Assoc. of America.

Ibragimov, I. A. & Hasminski, R. Z. [1982]. Bounds for the risk of nonparametric regression estimates. *Theory Prob. Appl.*, **28**, 81–94. (In Russian.)

Ibragimov, I. A. & Hasminski, R. Z. [1984]. On the nonparametric estimation of the value of a linear functional in Gaussian white noise. *Theory Prob. Appl.*, **29**, 19–32. (In Russian.)

Jackowski, T. & Woźniakowski, H. [1987]. Complexity of approximation with relative error criterion in worst, average and probabilistic settings. *J. Complexity*, **3**, 114–134.

Jaromczyk, J. W. & Wasilkowski, G. W. [1993]. Numerical stability of a convex hull algorithm for simple polygons. *Algorithmica*, **10**, 457–472.

Jaromczyk, J. W. & Wasilkowski, G. W. [1994]. Computing convex hull in floating point arithmetic. *Comput. Geometry: Theory Appl.*, **4**, 283–292.

Joy, C., Boyle, P. P., & Tan, K. S. [1996]. Quasi-Monte Carlo methods in numerical finance. *Management Sci.*, **42**(6), 706–938.

Judd, K. L. [1996]. Approximation, perturbation, and projection methods in economic analysis. *Pages 509–585 of:* Amman, H., Kendrick, D., & Rust, J. (eds), *Handbook of Computational Economics.* Handbooks in Econom., vol. 13. Amsterdam: Elsevier North-Holland.

Judd, K. L. [1997]. Asymptotic methods for aggregate growth models. *J. Economic Dynamics Control*, **21**, 1025–1042.

Judd, K. L. [1998]. *Numerical Methods in Economics.* Cambridge, MA: MIT Press.

Kacewicz, B. Z. [1987a]. Asymptotic error of algorithms for solving nonlinear problems. *J. Complexity*, **3**, 41–56.

Kacewicz, B. Z. [1987b]. Optimal solution of ordinary differential equations. *J. Complexity*, **3**, 451–465.

Kacewicz, B. Z. [1988]. Minimum asymptotic error of algorithms for solving ODE. *J. Complexity*, **4**, 373–389.

Kacewicz, B. Z. [1989]. How useful is nonadaptive information for ordinary differential equations? *Pages 41–47 of:* Milanese, M., Tempo, R., & Vicino, A. (eds), *Robustness in Identification and Control.* New York: Plenum.

Kacewicz, B. Z. [1990a]. On sequential and parallel solution of initial value problems. *J. Complexity*, **6**, 136–148.

Kacewicz, B. Z. [1990b]. Optimal solution of some two-point boundary value problem. *Pages 241–256 of: Numerical Analysis and Mathematical Methods*, vol. 24. Warsaw: Banach Center Publications.

Kacewicz, B. Z. [1996]. Solving linear problems in the presence of bounded data perturbations. *Pages 29–42 of:* Milanese, M., Norton, J. P., Piet-Lahanier, M., & Walter, E. (eds), *Bounding Approaches to System Identification*. New York: Plenum.

Kacewicz, B. Z. & Kowalski, M. A. [1991]. Recovering signals from inaccurate data. *Pages 68–74 of:* Silbermann, M. J. & Tagare, H. D. (eds), *Curves and Surfaces in Computer Vision and Graphics II*, vol. 1610. Boston, MA: International Society of Optical Engineering.

Kacewicz, B. Z. & Kowalski, M. A. [1995a]. Approximating linear functionals on unitary spaces in the presence of bounded data errors with applications to signal recovery. *Int. J. Adaptive Control Signal Processing*, **9**, 19–31.

Kacewicz, B. Z. & Kowalski, M. A. [1995b]. Recovering linear operators from inaccurate data. *J. Complexity*, **11**, 227–239.

Kacewicz, B. Z. & Milanese, M. [1995]. Optimality properties in finite sample l_1 identification with bounded noise. *Int. J. Adaptive Control Signal Processing*, **9**, 87–96.

Kacewicz, B. Z., Milanese, M., & Vicino, A. [1988]. Conditionally optimal algorithms and estimation of reduced order methods. *J. Complexity*, **4**(1), 73–85.

Kacewicz, B. Z. & Plaskota, L. [1990]. On the minimal cost of approximating linear problems based on information with deterministic noise. *Numer. Funct. Anal. Opt.*, **11**(5 and 6), 511–529.

Kacewicz, B. Z. & Plaskota, L. [1991]. Noisy information for linear problems in the asymptotic setting. *J. Complexity*, **7**, 35–57.

Kacewicz, B. Z. & Plaskota, L. [1992]. Termination conditions for approximating linear problems with noisy information. *Math. Comp.*, **59**(200), 503–513.

Kacewicz, B. Z. & Plaskota, L. [1993]. The minimal cost of approximating linear operators using perturbed information—the asymptotic setting. *J. Complexity*, **9**, 113–134.

Kadane, J. B. & Wasilkowski, G. W. [1985]. Average case ε-complexity: a Bayesian view. *Pages 361–374 of: Proceedings of II Valencia International Meeting on Bayesian Statistics*.

Kadane, J. B., Wasilkowski, G. W., & Woźniakowski, H. [1988]. On adaption with noisy information. *J. Complexity*, **4**, 257–276.

Karmarkar, N. [1984]. A new polynomial-time algorithm for linear programming. *Combinatorica*, **4**, 373–396.

Katscher, K., Novak, E., & Petras, K. [1996]. Quadrature formulas for multivariate convex functions. *J. Complexity*, **12**, 5–16.

Kearfott, R. B. [1987]. Abstract generalized bisection and a cost bound. *Math. Comp.*, **49**, 187–202.

Kearfott, R. B. [1996]. *Rigorous Global Search: Continuous Problems*. Dodrecht, Netherlands: Kluwer.

Keister, B. D. [1996]. Multidimensional quadrature algorithms. *Computers in Physics*, **10**(2), 119–122.

Keller, A. [1995]. A quasi-Monte Carlo algorithm for the global illumination problem in the Radiosity Setting. *Pages 239–251 of:* Niederreiter, H. & Shiue, P. (eds), *Monte Carlo and Quasi-Monte Carlo Methods in Scientific Computing*, vol. 106. New York: Springer-Verlag.

Keller, A. [1998]. *Quasi-Monte Carlo Methods for Photorealistic Image Synthesis*. Aachen: Shaker.

Khachian, L. G. [1979]. A polynomial algorithm in linear programming. *Soviet Math. Dokl.*, **20**, 191–194.

Kiefer, J. [1953]. Sequential minimax search for a maximum. *Proc. Amer. Math. Soc.*, **4**, 502–505.

Knuth, D. E. [1976]. Big omicron and big omega and big theta. *SIGACT News*, April.

Ko, K. I. [1991]. *Complexity Theory of Real Functions*. Basel: Birkhäuser.

Kolmogorov, A. N. [1955]. Evaluation of minimal number of elements of ε-nets in different functional classes and their application to the problem of representation of functions of several variables by superposition of functions of a smaller number of variables. *Usp. Mat. Nauk*, **10**(1), 192–194. (In Russian.)

Kolmogorov, A. N. & Tikhomirov, V. M. [1959]. ε-entropy and ε-capacity of sets in function space. *Usp. Mat. Nauk*, **14**(2), 3–86.

Kon, M. A. & Novak, E. [1989]. On the adaptive and continuous information problems. *J. Complexity*, **5**, 345–362.

Kon, M. A. & Novak, E. [1990]. The adaption problem for approximating linear operators. *Bull. Amer. Math. Soc.*, **23**, 159–165.

Kon, M. A., Ritter, K., & Werschulz, A. G. [1991]. On the average case solvability of ill-posed problems. *J. Complexity*, **7**, 220–224.

Kon, M. A. & Tempo, R. [1989]. On linearity of spline algorithms. *J. Complexity*, **5**, 251–259.

Korneichuk, N. P. [1994]. Optimization of active algorithms for recovery of monotonic functions from Hölder's class. *J. Complexity*, **10**, 265–269.

Kowalski, M. A. [1989]. On approximation of band-limited signals. *J. Complexity*, **5**, 283–302.

Kowalski, M. A., Sikorski, K., & Stenger, F. [1995]. *Selected Topics in Approximation and Computation*. New York: Oxford University Press.

Kuczyński, J. & Woźniakowski, H. [1992]. Estimating the largest eigenvalue by the power and Lanczos algorithms with a random start. *SIAM J. Matrix Anal. Appl.*, 1094–1122.

Kuczyński, J. & Woźniakowski, H. [1994]. Probabilistic bounds on the extremal eigenvalues and condition number by the Lanczos algorithm. *SIAM J. Matrix Anal. Appl.*, **15**(2), 672–691.

Kuo, H. H. [1975]. *Gaussian Measures in Banach Spaces*. Lecture Notes in Mathematics, vol. 463. New York: Springer-Verlag.

Larkin, F. M. [1972]. Gaussian measure in Hilbert space and application in numerical analysis. *Rocky Mount. J. Math.*, **2**, 372–421.

Lawler, E. [1980]. The great mathematical sputnik of 1979. *The Sciences*, **20**(7), 12–15.

Lee, D., Papageorgiou, A. F., & Wasilkowski, G. W. [1988]. Computational aspects of determining optical flow. *Pages 612–618 of: Proceedings of 2nd International Conference on Computer Vision.*

Lee, D., Papageorgiou, A. F., & Wasilkowski, G. W. [1989]. Computing optical flow. *Pages 99–106 of: Proceedings of IEEE Computer Society on Visual Motion.*

Lee, D., Pavlidis, T., & Wasilkowski, G. W. [1987]. A note on the trade-off between sampling and quantization in signal processing. *J. Complexity*, **3**, 359–371.

Lee, D. & Wasilkowski, G. W. [1986]. Discontinuity detection and thresholding—a stochastic approach. *J. Complexity*, **9**, 76–96.

Lee, D., Wasilkowski, G. W., & Mehrotra, R. [1993]. A new zero-crossing-based edge detector. *IEEE Trans. Image Processing*, **2**, 265–268.

Lee, D. & Woźniakowski, H. [1995a]. Testing linear operators. *BIT*, **35**, 331–351.

Lee, D. & Woźniakowski, H. [1995b]. Testing nonlinear operators. *Numer. Algorithms*, **9**, 319–342.

Lee, D. & Woźniakowski, H. [1997]. Testing linear operators: An average case analysis. *BIT*. (Submitted.)

Lee, D. & Yannakakis, M. [1994]. Testing finite state machines: state identification and verification. *IEEE Trans. Comput.*, **43**(3), 306–320.

Lee, D. & Yannakakis, M. [1995]. Testing finite state machines: fault detection. *J. Comp. System Sci.*, **50**(2), 209–227.

Lloyd, S. [1996]. *Measures of Complexity*. Department of Mechanical Engineering, Massachusetts Institute of Technology, Cambridge, MA.

Lord, G., Paskov, S. H., & Vanderhoof, I. T. [1996]. Using low-discrepancy points to value complex financial instruments. *Contingencies*, **8**(5), 52–56.

Lynch, N. A. & Lundelius, J. [1985]. An upper and lower bound for clock synchronization. *Inform. Control*, **62**(2/3), 190–204.

Magaril-Il'yaev, G. G. [1994]. Average widths of Sobolev classes on $\mathbb{R}^n$. *J. Approx. Theory*, **76**, 65–76.

Magaril-Il'yaev, G. G. & Osipenko, K. Yu. [1991]. On optimal recovery of functionals from inaccurate data. *Mat. Zametki*, **50**, 85–93. (In Russian.)

Maiorov, V. [1993]. Average n-widths of the Wiener space in the L_∞-norm. *J. Complexity*, **9**, 222–230.

Maiorov, V. [1994]. Linear widths of function spaces equipped with the Gaussian measure. *J. Approx. Theory*, **77**, 74–88.

Maiorov, V. & Wasilkowski, G. W. [1995]. Probabilistic and average linear widths in L_∞-norm with respect to r-fold Wiener measure. *J. Approx. Theory*, **84**, 31–40.

Marchuk, A. G. & Osipenko, K. Yu. [1975]. Best approximation of functions specified with an error at a finite number of points. *Math. Notes*, **17**, 207–212.

Marr, D. [1981]. *Vision: A Computational Investigation in the Human Representation and Processing of Visual Information.* San Francisco: W. H. Freeman.

Mathé, P. [1990]. s-Numbers in information-based complexity. *J. Complexity*, **6**, 41–66.

Mathé, P. [1991]. Random approximation of Sobolev embeddings. *J. Complexity*, **7**, 261–281.

Mathé, P. [1993a]. A minimax principle for the optimal error of Monte Carlo methods. *Constr. Approx.*, **9**, 23–29.

Mathé, P. [1993b]. On optimal random nets. *J. Complexity*, **9**, 171–180.

Mathé, P. [1994]. *Approximation theory of stochastic numerical methods.* Habilitation thesis, Institut für Angewandte Analysis und Stochastic, Berlin.

Mathé, P. [1995]. The optimal error of Monte Carlo integration. *J. Complexity*, **11**(4), 394–415.

Mathé, P. [1996]. Optimal reconstruction of stochastic evolutions. *Pages 523–532 of:* Renegar, J., Shub, M., & Smale, S. (eds), *The Mathematics of Numerical Analysis.* Lectures in Applied Mathematics, vol. 32. Providence, RI: Amer. Math. Soc.

Megiddo, N. [1983]. Towards a genuinely polynomial algorithm for linear programming. *SIAM J. Comp.*, **12**(2), 347–353.

Melkman, A. A. & Micchelli, C. A. [1979]. Optimal estimation of linear operators in Hilbert spaces from inaccurate data. *SIAM J. Numer. Anal.*, **16**, 87–105.

Metropolis, N. & Ulam, S. [1949]. The Monte Carlo method. *J. Amer. Statist. Assoc.*, **44**, 335–341.

Micchelli, C. A. [1989]. Optimal sampling design for parametric estimation and p-widths under stochastic and deterministic noise. *Pages 25–40 of:* Milanese, M., Tempo, R., & Vicino, A. (eds), *Robustness in Identification and Control.* New York: Plenum.

Micchelli, C. A. [1993]. Optimal estimation of linear operators from inaccurate data: a second look. *Numer. Algorithms*, **5**, 375–390.

Micchelli, C. A., Cavaretta, A. S., & Sharma, A. [1992]. Walsh equiconvergence theorem and optimal recovery. *Anal.*, **12**, 271–302.

Micchelli, C. A. & Fisher, S. D. [1997]. Minimal norm interpolation with nonnegative real part on multiply connected planar domains. *Michigan Math. Monthly*, 167–181.

Micchelli, C. A. & Rivlin, T. J. [1977]. A survey of optimal recovery. *Pages 1–54 of: Optimal Estimation in Approximation Theory.* New York: Plenum.

Micchelli, C. A. & Rivlin, T. J. [1987]. An optimal recovery view of Walsh's equiconvergence theorem. *J. Complexity*, **3**, 312–330.

Micchelli, C. A. & Wahba, G. [1981]. Design problems for optimal surface interpolation. *Pages 329–347 of:* Ziegler, Z. (ed), *Approximation Theory and Applications.* New York: Academic Press.

Milanese, M. & Belforte, G. [1982]. Estimation theory and uncertainty interval evaluation in presence of unknown but bounded errors: linear families of models and estimators. *IEEE Trans. Auto. Control*, **AC-27**, 408–414.

Milanese, M. & Kacewicz, B. Z. [1994]. Error bounds in finite samples worst-case l_1 identification. *Pages 33–42 of:* Kurzhanski, A. B. & Veliov, V. M. (eds), *Modeling Techniques for Uncertain Systems.* Basel: Birkhäuser.

Milanese, M. & Tempo, R. [1985]. Optimal algorithms theory for robust estimation and prediction. *IEEE Trans. Auto. Control*, **30**, 730–738.

Milanese, M., Tempo, R., & Vicino, A. [1986]. Strongly optimal algorithms and optimal information in estimation problems. *J. Complexity*, **2**, 78–94.

Milanese, M., Tempo, R., & Vicino, A. (eds) [1989]. *Robustness in Identification and Control.* New York: Plenum.

Moore, E. F. [1956]. Gedanken-experiments on sequential machines. *Pages*

129–153 of: Automata Studies. Annals of Mathematics Studies, no. 34. Princeton, NJ: Princeton University Press.

Morokoff, W. J. & Caflisch, R. E. [1995]. Quasi-Monte Carlo integration. *J. Comp. Phys.*, **122**, 218–230.

Morozov, V. A. [1984]. *Methods for Solving Incorrectly Posed Problems.* New York: Springer-Verlag.

Mount, K. & Reiter, S. [1990]. *A model of computing with human agents.* Center for Mathematical Studies in Economics and Management Science, Discussion Paper 890. Northwestern University, Evanston, IL.

Natarajan, B. K. [1993]. Condition-sensitive computation of approximate fixed points. *J. Complexity*, **9**, 406–411.

Nemirovsky, A. S. [1992]. Information-based complexity of linear operator equations. *J. Complexity*, **8**, 93–123.

Nemirovsky, A. S. [1994]. On parallel complexity of nonsmooth convex optimization. *J. Complexity*, **10**, 451–463.

Nemirovsky, A. S. & Nesterov, Y. [1994]. *Interior-Point Polynomial Algorithms in Convex Programming.* Philadelphia: SIAM.

Nemirovsky, A. S. & Yudin, D. B. [1976]. A bound of information complexity for mathematical programming problems. *Ekonom. Mat. Metody*, **12**, 128–142. (In Russian.)

Nemirovsky, A. S. & Yudin, D. B. [1983]. *Problem Complexity and Method Efficiency in Optimization.* New York: Wiley-Interscience.

Niederreiter, H. [1978]. Quasi-Monte Carlo methods and pseudo-random numbers. *Bull. Amer. Math. Soc. (New Ser.)*, **84**, 957–1041.

Niederreiter, H. [1992]. *Random Number Generation and Quasi-Monte Carlo Methods.* CBMS-NSF Regional Conference Series in Applied Mathematics. Philadelphia: SIAM.

Nikolskij, S. M. [1950]. On the problem of approximation estimate by quadrature formulae. *Usp. Mat. Nauk*, **5**, 165–177. (In Russian.)

Ninomiya, S. & Tezuka, S. [1996]. Toward real-time pricing of complex financial derivatives. *Appl. Math. Finance*, **3**, 1–20.

Novak, E. [1988a]. *Deterministic and Stochastic Error Bounds in Numerical Analysis.* Lecture Notes in Mathematics, vol. 1349. New York: Springer-Verlag.

Novak, E. [1988b]. Stochastic properties of quadrature formulas. *Numer. Math.*, **53**(5), 609–620.

Novak, E. [1989]. Average case results for zero finding. *J. Complexity*, **5**, 489–501.

Novak, E. [1991]. Determining zeroes of increasing Lipschitz functions. *Aeq. Math.*, **41**, 161–167.

Novak, E. [1992]. Quadrature formulas for monotone functions. *Proc. Amer. Math. Soc.*, **115**, 59–68.

Novak, E. [1993]. Quadrature formulas for convex classes of functions. *Pages 283–296 of:* Brass, H. & Hämmerlin, G. (eds), *Numerical Integration IV.* Basel: Birkhäuser.

Novak, E. [1995a]. The adaption problem for nonsymmetric convex sets. *J. Approx. Theory*, **82**, 123–134.

Novak, E. [1995b]. The Bayesian approach to numerical problems: results for zero finding. *Pages 164–171 of: Proceedings IMACS-GAMM International Symposium on Numerical Methods and Error Bounds.* Berlin: Akademie Verlag.

Novak, E. [1995c]. The real number model in numerical analysis. *J. Complexity*, **11**, 57–73.

Novak, E. [1996]. On the power of adaption. *J. Complexity*, **12**(3), 199–237.

Novak, E. & Petras, K. [1994]. Optimal stochastic quadrature formulas for convex functions. *BIT*, **34**, 288–294.

Novak, E. & Ritter, K. [1989]. A stochastic analog to Chebyshev centers and optimal average case algorithms. *J. Complexity*, **5**, 60–79.

Novak, E. & Ritter, K. [1992]. Average errors for zero finding: lower bounds. *Math. Z.*, **211**, 671–686.

Novak, E. & Ritter, K. [1993]. Some complexity results for zero finding for univariate functions. *J. Complexity*, **9**, 15–40.

Novak, E. & Ritter, K. [1996a]. The curse of dimension and a universal method for numerical integration. Nürnberger, G., Schmidt, J. W., & Walz, G. (eds), *Multivariate Approximation and Splines*. International Series in Numerical Mathematics. Basel: Birkhäuser.

Novak, E. & Ritter, K. [1996b]. Global optimization using hyperbolic cross points. *Pages 19–33 of:* Floudas, C. A. & Pardalos, P. M. (eds), *State of the Art in Global Optimization: Computational Methods and Applications*. Dordrecht, Netherlands: Kluwer.

Novak, E. & Ritter, K. [1996c]. High dimensional integration of smooth functions over cubes. *Numer. Math.*, **75**, 79–97.

Novak, E., Ritter, K., & Woźniakowski, H. [1995]. Average-case optimality of a hybrid secant-bisection method. *Math. Comp.*, **64**(212), 1517–1539.

Novak, E., Sloan, I. H., & Woźniakowski, H. [1997]. Tractabillity of tensor product linear operators. *J. Complexity*, **13**, 387–418.

Novak, E. & Woźniakowski, H. [1992]. Relaxed verification for continuous problems. *J. Complexity*, **8**, 124–152.

Novak, E. & Woźniakowski, H. [1996]. Topological complexity of zero finding. *J. Complexity*, **12**, 380–400.

Osipenko, K. Yu. [1996]. Optimal recovery of periodic functions from Fourier coefficients given with an error. *J. Complexity*, **12**, 35–46.

Ostrowski, A. M. [1954]. On two problems in abstract algebra connected with Horner's rule. *Pages 40–48 of:* Taussky-Todd, O. (ed), *Studies in Mathematics and Mechanics Presented to Richard von Mises*. New York: Academic Press.

Owen, A. B. [1995]. Randomly permuted (t, m, s)-nets and (t, s)-sequences. *Pages 299–317 of:* Niederreiter, H. & Shiue, P. (eds), *Monte Carlo and Quasi-Monte Carlo Methods in Scientific Computing*. New York: Springer-Verlag.

Owen, A. B. [1997]. Monte Carlo variance of scrambled net quadrature. *SIAM J. Numer. Anal.*, **34**. 1884–1910.

Packel, E. W. [1988]. Do linear problems have linear optimal algorithms? *SIAM Rev.*, **30**(3), 388–403.

Packel, E. W. & Traub, J. F. [1987]. Information-based complexity. *Nature*, **328**, 29–33.

Packel, E. W., Traub, J. F., & Woźniakowski, H. [1992]. Measures of uncertainty and information in computation. *Inform. Sci.*, **65**, 253–273.

Packel, E. W. & Woźniakowski, H. [1987]. Recent developments in information-based complexity. *Bull. Amer. Math. Soc.*, **17**, 9–36.

Papadimitriou, C. H. & Tsitsiklis, J. N. [1986]. Intractable problems in control theory. *SIAM J. Control Opt.*, **24**, 639–654.

Papageorgiou, A. F. [1989]. *Average case complexity bounds for continuous problems.* Ph.D. thesis, Columbia University, Department of Computer Science, New York.

Papageorgiou, A. F. [1993]. Integration of monotone functions of several variables. *J. Complexity,* **9**, 252–268.

Papageorgiou, A. F. [1998]. Work in progress.

Papageorgiou, A. F. & Traub, J. F. [1996]. Beating Monte Carlo. *Risk,* **9**(6), 63–65.

Papageorgiou, A. F. & Traub, J. F. [1997]. Faster evaluation of multidimensional integrals. *Comp. Phys.,* **11**(6), 574–578.

Papageorgiou, A. F. & Wasilkowski, G. W. [1990]. On the average complexity of multivariate problems. *J. Complexity,* **6**, 1–23.

Paskov, S. H. [1992]. Singularity of bivariate interpolation. *J. Approx. Theory,* **70**(1), 50–67.

Paskov, S. H. [1993]. Average case complexity of multivariate integration for smooth functions. *J. Complexity,* **9**(2), 291–312.

Paskov, S. H. [1995a]. *Analysis of Multivariate Problems with Applications to Finance.* Ph.D. thesis, Columbia University, Department of Computer Science, New York.

Paskov, S. H. [1995b]. Termination Criteria for Linear Problems. *J. Complexity,* **11**, 105–137.

Paskov, S. H. [1997]. New methodologies for valuing derivatives. *Pages 545–582 of:* Pliska, S. & Dempster, M. (eds), *Mathematics of Derivative Securities.* Cambridge: Cambridge University Press. (This is a slightly modified version of a 1994 Columbia University Computer Science Department Technical Report.)

Paskov, S. H. & Traub, J. F. [1995]. Faster valuation of financial derivatives. *J. Portfolio Management,* **22**(1), 113–120.

Penrose, R. L. [1989]. *The Emperor's New Mind.* Oxford: Oxford University Press.

Pereverzev, S. V. [1988]. On the complexity of the problem of finding the solutions of Fredholm equations of the second kind with smooth kernels I. *Ukrain. Mat. Zh.,* **40**(1), 84–91. (In Russian.)

Pereverzev, S. V. [1989]. On the complexity of the problem of finding the solutions of Fredholm equations of the second kind with smooth kernels II. *Ukrain. Mat. Zh.,* **41**(2), 189–193. (In Russian.)

Pereverzev, S. V. [1991]. Hyperbolic cross and complexity of an approximate solution of Fredholm integral equations of the second kind with differentiable kernels. *Sibirsk. Mat. Zh.,* **32**(1), 107–115. (In Russian.)

Pereverzev, S. V. [1992]. Complexity of the Fredholm problem of second kind. *Pages 255–272 of: Optimal Recovery.* New York: Nova Science.

Pereverzev, S. V. [1996]. *Optimization of Methods of Approximate Solution of Operator Equations.* New York: Nova Science.

Pereverzev, S. V. & Azizov, M. [1996]. On optimal methods of defining information for solution of integral equations with analytic kernels. *Ukrain. Mat. Zh.,* **48**(5), 656–664. (In Russian.)

Pereverzev, S. V. & Makhkamov, K. Sh. [1991]. Galerkin information, hyperbolic cross and the complexity of operator equations. *Ukrain. Mat. Zh.,* **43**(5), 639–648. (In Russian.)

Pereverzev, S. V. & Scharipov, C. C. [1992]. Information complexity of equations of the second kind with compact operators in Hilbert space.

J. Complexity, **8**(2), 176–202.

Pereverzev, S. V. & Solodky, S. G. [1996]. The minimal radius of Galerkin information for the Fredholm problem of the first kind. *J. Complexity*, **12**, 401–415.

Petras, K. [1994]. Quadrature errors for functions with derivatives of bounded variation. *J. Comp. Inform.*, **4**, 123–143.

Petras, K. [1996]. On the universality of the Gaussian quadrature formula. *East J. Approx.*, **2**, 427–438.

Petras, K. [1998]. Gaussian versus optimal integration of analytic functions. *Constr. Approx.* (To appear.)

Pinkus, A. [1981]. Best approximation by smooth functions. *J. Approx. Theory*, **33**, 147–178.

Pinkus, A. [1985]. *n-Widths in Approximation Theory*. New York: Springer-Verlag.

Plaskota, L. [1989a]. Asymptotic error for the global maximum of functions in s-dimensions. *J. Complexity*, **5**, 369–378.

Plaskota, L. [1989b]. On complexity of computations. *Delta*, **18**. (In Polish.)

Plaskota, L. [1990]. On average case complexity of linear problems with noisy information. *J. Complexity*, **6**, 199–230.

Plaskota, L. [1992]. Function approximation and integration on the Wiener space with noisy data. *J. Complexity*, **8**, 301–323.

Plaskota, L. [1993a]. A note on varying cardinality in the average case setting. *J. Complexity*, **9**, 458–470.

Plaskota, L. [1993b]. Optimal approximation of linear operators based on noisy data on functionals. *J. Approx. Theory*, **73**, 93–105.

Plaskota, L. [1994]. Average case approximation of linear functionals based on information with deterministic noise. *J. Comp. Inform.*, **4**, 21–39.

Plaskota, L. [1995]. Average complexity for linear problems in a model with varying information noise. *J. Complexity*, **11**, 240–264.

Plaskota, L. [1996a]. Complexity of problems with noisy information. *Z. Angew. Math. Mech.*, **3**, 116–120. Presented at ICIAM/GAMM 95, July 3–7, 1995, Hamburg.

Plaskota, L. [1996b]. How to benefit from noise. *J. Complexity*, **12**(2), 175–184.

Plaskota, L. [1996c]. *Noisy Information and Computational Complexity*. Cambridge: Cambridge University Press.

Plaskota, L. [1996d]. Survey of computational complexity with noisy information. *Pages 651–664 of:* Renegar, J., Shub, M., & Smale, S. (eds), *The Mathematics of Numerical Analysis*. Lectures in Applied Mathematics, vol. 32. Providence, RI: Amer. Math. Soc.

Plaskota, L. [1996e]. Worst case complexity of problems with random information noise. *J. Complexity*, **12**, 416–439.

Plaskota, L. [1998]. Average case L_∞-approximation in the presence of Gaussian noise. *J. Approx. Theory*. (To appear.)

Plaskota, L., Wasilkowski, G. W., & Woźniakowski, H. [1998]. *A new algorithm and worst case complexity for Feynman-Kac path integration.* (In preparation.)

Pour-El, M. B. & Richards, J. I. [1988]. *Computability in Analysis and Physics*. New York: Springer-Verlag.

Press, W., Teukolsky, S., Vetterling, W., & Flannery, B. [1992]. *Numerical Recipes in C*. Second edn. Cambridge: Cambridge University Press.

Rabin, M. A. [1972]. Solving linear equations by means of scalar products. *Pages 11–20 of:* Miller, R. E. & Thatcher, J. W. (eds), *Complexity of Computer Computations.* New York: Plenum.

Radner, R. [1993]. The organization of decentralized infomration processing. *Econometrica,* **62**, 1109–1146.

Reiter, S. & Simon, C. [1992]. A decentralized dynamic process for finding equilibrium. *J. Econom. Theory,* **56**, 400–425.

Renegar, J. [1987]. On the worst case arithmetic complexity of approximating zeros of polynomials. *J. Complexity,* **3**, 90–113.

Renegar, J. [1988]. A polynomial-time algorithm, based on Newton's method, for linear programming. *Math. Programming,* **40**(1), 59–93.

Renegar, J. [1989]. On the worst case arithmetic complexity of approximating zeros of systems of polynomials. *SIAM J. Comp.,* **18**, 350–370.

Renegar, J. [1992a]. On the computational complexity and geometry of the first-order theory of the reals: Parts I, II and III. *J. Symb. Comp.,* **13**, 255–352.

Renegar, J. [1992b]. On the computational complexity of approximating solutions for real algebraic formulae. *SIAM J. Comp.,* **21**, 1008–1025.

Renegar, J., Shub, M., & Smale, S. (eds) [1996]. *The Mathematics of Numerical Analysis.* Lectures in Applied Mathematics, vol. 32. Providence, RI: Amer. Math. Soc.

Ritter, K. [1994]. Average errors for zero finding: lower bounds for smooth or monotone functions. *Aeq. Math.,* **48**(2–3), 194–219.

Ritter, K. [1996a]. Almost optimal differentiation using noisy data. *J. Approx. Theory,* **86**(3), 293–309.

Ritter, K. [1996b]. *Average case analysis of numerical problems.* Habilitation thesis, Universität Erlangen-Nürnberg, Germany.

Ritter, K. & Wasilkowski, G. W. [1996a]. Integration and L_2-approximation: average case setting with isotropic Wiener measure for smooth functions. *Rocky Mount. J. Math.,* **26**, 1541–1557.

Ritter, K. & Wasilkowski, G. W. [1996b]. On the average complexity of solving Poisson equations. *Pages 677–687 of:* Renegar, J., Shub, M., & Smale, S. (eds), *The Mathematics of Numerical Analysis.* Lectures in Applied Mathematics, vol. 32. Providence, RI: Amer. Math. Soc.

Ritter, K., Wasilkowski, G. W., & Woźniakowski, H. [1993]. On multivariate integration of stochastic processes. *Pages 331–347 of:* Brass, H. & Hämmerlin, G. (eds), *Numerical Integration IV.* Basel: Birkhäuser.

Ritter, K., Wasilkowski, G. W., & Woźniakowski, H. [1995]. Multivariate integration and approximation for random fields satisfying Sacks-Ylvisaker conditions. *Ann. Appl. Prob.,* **5**, 518–541.

Roth, K. F. [1954]. On irregularities of distribution. *Mathematika,* **1**, 73–79.

Roth, K. F. [1980]. On irregularities of distribution, IV. *Acta Arithmetica,* **37**, 67–75.

Rust, J. [1996]. Numerical dynamic programming in economics. *Pages 619–729 of:* Amman, H., Kendrick, D., & Rust, J. (eds), *Handbook of Computational Economics.* Handbooks in Econom., vol. 13. Amsterdam: Elsevier North-Holland.

Rust, J. [1997]. Using randomization to break the curse of dimensionality. *Econometrica,* **65**(3), 487–516.

Sacks, J. & Ylvisaker, D. [1966]. Designs for regression with correlated errors. *Ann. Math. Statist.*, **37**, 68–89.

Sard, A. [1949]. Best approximate integration formulas: best approximation formulas. *Amer. J. Math.*, **71**, 80–91.

Schoenberg, I. J. [1964]. Spline interpolation and best quadrature formulas. *Bull. Amer. Math. Soc.*, **70**, 143–148.

Shannon, C. E. [1948]. A mathematical theory of communication. *Bell Sys. Tech. J.*, **27**, 379–423, 623–656.

Shub, M., Bürgisser, P., & Lickteig, T. [1992]. Test complexity of generic polynomials. *J. Complexity*, **8**, 203–215.

Shub, M. & Smale, S. [1986]. On the existence of generally convergent algorithms. *J. Complexity*, **2**, 2–11.

Shub, M. & Smale, S. [1993a]. Complexity of Bezout's theorem I: geometrical aspects. *J. Amer. Math. Soc.*, **6**, 459–501.

Shub, M. & Smale, S. [1993b]. Complexity of Bezout's theorem II: volumes and probabilities. *Pages 267–285 of:* Eyssette, F. & Galligo, A. (eds), *Computational Algebraic Geometry.* Progress in Mathematics, vol. 109. Basel: Birkhäuser.

Shub, M. & Smale, S. [1993c]. Complexity of Bezout's theorem III: condition number and packing. *J. Complexity*, **9**, 4–14.

Shub, M. & Smale, S. [1994]. Complexity of Bezout's theorem V: polynomial time. *Theoret. Comp. Sci.*, **133**, 141–164.

Shub, M. & Smale, S. [1995]. On the intractability of Hilbert's Nullstellensatz and an algebraic version of "NP $\neq$ P?". *Duke Math. J.*, **81**, 47–54.

Shub, M. & Smale, S. [1996]. Complexity of Bezout's theorem IV: probability of success; extensions. *SIAM J. Numer. Anal.*, **33**, 128–148.

Shub, M., Tischler, D., & Williams, R. F. [1988]. The Newtonian graph of a complex polynomial. *SIAM J. Math. Anal.*, **19**, 246–256.

Sikorski, K. [1985]. Optimal solution of nonlinear equations. *J. Complexity*, **1**, 197–209.

Sikorski, K. [1989a]. Fast algorithms for the computation of fixed points. *Pages 49–59 of:* Milanese, M., Tempo, R., & Vicino, A. (eds), *Robustness in Identification and Control.* New York: Plenum.

Sikorski, K. [1989b]. Study of linear information for classes of polynomial equations. *Aeq. Math.*, **37**, 1–14.

Sikorski, K. [1998]. *Optimal Solution of Nonlinear Equations.* Oxford: Oxford University Press.

Sikorski, K. & Trojan, G. M. [1990]. Asymptotic near optimality of the bisection method. *Numer. Math.*, **57**, 421–433.

Sikorski, K., Tsay, C. W., & Woźniakowski, H. [1993]. An ellipsoid algorithm for the computation of fixed points. *J. Complexity*, 181–200.

Sikorski, K. & Woźniakowski, H. [1986]. For which error criterion can we solve nonlinear equations? *J. Complexity*, **2**, 163–178.

Sikorski, K. & Woźniakowski, H. [1987]. Complexity of fixed points I. *J. Complexity*, **3**, 388–405.

Skorohod, A. V. [1974]. *Integration in Hilbert Space.* New York: Springer-Verlag.

Sloan, I. H. & Joe, S. [1994]. *Lattice methods for multiple integration.* Oxford: Oxford University Press.

Sloan, I. H. & Woźniakowski, H. [1998a]. An intractability result for multiple integration. *Math. Comp.* (To appear.)

Sloan, I. H. & Woźniakowski, H. [1998b]. When are quasi-Monte Carlo algorithms efficient for high dimensional integrals? *J. Complexity*, **14**, 1–33.

Smolyak, S. A. [1963]. Quadrature and interpolation formulas for tensor products of certain classes of functions. *Dokl. Akad. Nauk SSSR*, **4**, 240–243. (In Russian.)

Smolyak, S. A. [1965]. *On optimal recovery of functions and functionals of them.* Ph.D. thesis, Moscow State Univ., Moscow. (In Russian.)

Sobol', I. M. [1967]. The distribution of points in a cube and the approximate evaluation of integrals. *USSR Comp. Math. Math. Phys.*, **7**(4), 86–112.

Solodky, S. G. [1994]. Optimization of algorithms for the approximate solution of the Volterra equations with infinitely differentiable kernels. *Ukrain. Mat. Zh.*, **46**(11), 1534–1545. (In Russian.)

Solodky, S. G. [1996]. Complexity of the second kind Fredholm equations with kernels belonging to anisotropic classes of differentiable functions. *Ukrain. Mat. Zh.*, **48**(4), 525–532. (In Russian.)

Strassen, V. [1969]. Gaussian elimination is not optimal. *Numer. Math.*, **13**, 354–356.

Sukharev, A. G. [1986]. On the existence of optimal affine methods for approximating linear functionals. *J. Complexity*, **2**, 317–322.

Suldin, A. V. [1959]. Wiener measure and its applications to approximation methods I. *Izv. Vyssh. Uchebn. Zaved. Mat.*, **13**, 145–158. (In Russian.)

Suldin, A. V. [1960]. Wiener measure and its applications to approximation methods II. *Izv. Vyssh. Uchebn. Zaved. Mat.*, **18**, 165–179. (In Russian.)

Sun, Y. & Wang, C. [1994]. μ-Average n-widths on the Wiener space. *J. Complexity*, **10**, 428–436.

Tardos, E. [1986]. A strongly polynomial algorithm to solve combinatorial linear programs. *Oper. Res.*, **34**(2), 250–256.

Temlyakov, V. N. [1987]. Approximate recovery of periodic functions of several variables. *Math. USSR Sbornik*, **56**, 249–261.

Temlyakov, V. N. [1989]. Approximation of functions with bounded mixed derivatives. *Proc. Steklov Inst. Math*, **178**, 1–121.

Temlyakov, V. N. [1990]. On an approach of obtaining lower bonds for the error of quadratures. *Math. USSR Sbornik*, **71**(1), 247–257.

Temlyakov, V. N. [1993]. On approximate recovery of functions with bounded mixed derivatives. *J. Complexity*, **9**(1), 41–59.

Tempo, R. [1992]. IBC: a working tool for robust parametric identification. *Pages 237–240 of: Proceedings of the 1992 American Control Conference*. Piscataway, NJ: IEEE Press.

Tempo, R. [1995]. Worst-case optimality of smoothing algorithms for parametric system identification. *Automatica*, **31**, 759–763.

Tempo, R. & Cerone, V. [1992]. Robust stability: the computational complexity point of view. *J. Complexity*, **8**, 265–276.

Tempo, R. & Wasilkowski, G. W. [1988]. Maximum likelihood estimators and worst case optimal algorithms for system identification. *Sys. Control Lett.*, **10**(4), 265–270.

Tezuka, S. [1995]. *Uniform Random Numbers: Theory and Practice.* Dordrecht, Netherlands: Kluwer.

Traub, J. F. [1961]. On functional iteration and calculation of roots. *Pages 1–4 in Session 5A-1 of: Preprints of Papers 16th Nat. ACM Conf.* Association for Computing Machinery, Los Angeles.

Traub, J. F. [1964]. *Iterative Methods for the Solution of Equations.* Englewood Cliffs, NJ: Prentice-Hall.

Traub, J. F. [1985a]. Complexity of approximately solved problems. *J. Complexity,* **1**, 3–10.

Traub, J. F. [1985b]. *Information, complexity, and the sciences.* University Lecture, Columbia University, New York.

Traub, J. F. [1988]. Introduction to information-based complexity. *Pages 62–76 of:* Abu-Mostafa, Y. S. (ed), *Complexity in Information Theory.* New York: Springer-Verlag.

Traub, J. F. [1991]. What is scientifically knowable? *Pages 489–503 of:* Rashid, R. F. (ed), *CMU Computer Science: A Twenty-Fifth Anniversary Commemorative.* Reading, MA: Addison-Wesley.

Traub, J. F. [1996]. On reality and models. *Pages 238–254 of:* Casti, J. & Karlqvist, A. (eds), *Boundaries and Barriers: On the Limits to Scientific Knowledge.* Reading, MA: Addison-Wesley.

Traub, J. F. [1997]. Do negative results from formal systems limit scientific knowledge? *Complexity,* **3**(1), 29–31.

Traub, J. F., Wasilkowski, G. W., & Woźniakowski, H. [1983]. *Information, Uncertainty, Complexity.* Reading, MA: Addison-Wesley.

Traub, J. F., Wasilkowski, G. W., & Woźniakowski, H. [1988]. *Information-Based Complexity.* New York: Academic Press.

Traub, J. F. & Werschulz, A. G. [1994]. Linear ill-posed problems are solvable on the average for all Gaussian measures. *Math. Intelligencer,* **16**(2), 42–48.

Traub, J. F. & Woźniakowski, H. [1976]. Strict lower and upper bounds on iterative computational complexity. *Pages 15–34 of:* Traub, J. F. (ed), *Analytic Computational Complexity.* New York: Academic Press.

Traub, J. F. & Woźniakowski, H. [1979]. *On a Soviet algorithm for the linear programming problem.* Tech. rept. Columbia University Computer Science Department, New York.

Traub, J. F. & Woźniakowski, H. [1980]. *A General Theory of Optimal Algorithms.* ACM Monograph Series. New York: Academic Press.

Traub, J. F. & Woźniakowski, H. [1982]. Complexity of linear programming. *Oper. Res. Lett.,* **1**, 59–62.

Traub, J. F. & Woźniakowski, H. [1984]. On the optimal solution of large linear systems. *J. Assoc. Comp. Mach.,* **31**, 545–559.

Traub, J. F. & Woźniakowski, H. [1991a]. Information-based complexity: new questions for mathematicians. *Mathematical Intelligencer,* **13**, 34–43.

Traub, J. F. & Woźniakowski, H. [1991b]. Theory and applications of information-based complexity. *Pages 163–193 of:* Nadel, L. & Stein, D. (eds), *1990 Lectures in Complex Systems.* Redwood City, CA: Addison-Wesley.

Traub, J. F. & Woźniakowski, H. [1992]. The Monte Carlo algorithm with a pseudorandom generator. *Math. Comp.,* **58**(197), 323–339.

Traub, J. F. & Woźniakowski, H. [1993]. Recent progress in information-based complexity. *Bull. EATCS,* 141–154.

Traub, J. F. & Woźniakowski, H. [1994]. Breaking intractabililty. *Sci. Amer.,* **270**, 102–107.

Tsay, C. W. [1994]. *Fixed Point Computation and Parallel Algorithms for Solving Wave Equations.* Ph.D. thesis, University of Utah.

Tsitsiklis, J. N. & Van Roy, B. [1997]. An analysis of temporal-difference learning with function approximation. *IEEE Trans. Auto. Control*, **42**(5), 674–690.

Turing, A. M. [1937]. Computable numbers, with an application to the Entscheidungsproblem. *Proc. London Math. Soc.*, **42**, 230–265.

Vakhania, N. N. [1991]. Gaussian mean boundedness of densely defined linear operators. *J. Complexity*, **7**, 225–231.

Vakhania, N. N., Tarieladze, V. I., & Chobanyan, S. A. [1987]. *Probability Distributions on Banach Spaces*. Dordrecht, Netherlands: Kluwer.

van Emde Boas, P. [1990]. Machine models and simulations. *Pages 1–66 of:* van Leeuwen, J. (ed), *Handbook of Theoretical Computer Science: Volume A, Algorithms and Complexity*. Cambridge, MA: MIT Press.

Van Zandt, T. [1998]. Decentralized information processing in the theory of organizations. Sertel, M. (ed), *Contemporary Economic Development Reviewed, Volume 4: The Enterprise and its Environment*. London: Macmillan. (Forthcoming.)

Vavasis, S. A. [1991]. *Nonlinear Optimization: Complexity Issues*. New York: Oxford University Press.

Vicino, A., Tempo, R., Genesio, R., & Milanese, M. [1987]. Optimal error and GMDH predictors: a comparison with some statistical techniques. *Int. J. Forecasting*, 313–328.

von Neumann, J. [1961]. The general and logical theory of automata. *Pages 288–328 of:* Taub, A. H. (ed), *Collected Works*, vol. V. London: Macmillan.

Wahba, G. [1971]. On the regression design problem of Sacks and Ylvisaker. *Ann. Math. Stat.*, **42**, 1035–1043.

Wahba, G. [1974]. Regression design for some equivalence classes of kernels. *Ann. Stat.*, **2**, 925–934.

Wahba, G. [1990]. *Spline Models for Observational Data*. Philadelphia: SIAM.

Wasilkowski, G. W. [1982]. The strength of nonstationary iteration. *Aeq. Math.*, **24**, 243–260.

Wasilkowski, G. W. [1983]. *Local average errors*. Tech. rept. Department of Computer Science, Columbia University, New York.

Wasilkowski, G. W. [1986]. Information of varying cardinality. *J. Complexity*, **2**, 204–228.

Wasilkowski, G. W. [1989a]. A clock synchronization problem with random delays. *J. Complexity*, **5**(1), 1–11.

Wasilkowski, G. W. [1989b]. On adaptive information with varying cardinality for linear problems with elliptically contoured measures. *J. Complexity*, **5**, 363–368.

Wasilkowski, G. W. [1989c]. Randomization for continuous problems. *J. Complexity*, **5**, 195–218.

Wasilkowski, G. W. [1990a]. Information-based complexity; an overview. *Pages 374–379 of: Proceedings of the 1990 American Control Conference*. Piscataway, NJ: IEEE Press.

Wasilkowski, G. W. [1990b]. Note on quantization for signals with bounded $(r + 1)$st derivative. *J. Complexity*, **6**, 278–289.

Wasilkowski, G. W. [1990c]. On piecewise-polynomial approximation for functions with a fractional derivative bounded in L_p-norm. *J. Approx. Theory*, **62**, 372–380.

Wasilkowski, G. W. [1992a]. On a posteriori upper bounds for approximating linear functionals in probabilistic setting. *J. Complexity*, **8**, 285–304.

Wasilkowski, G. W. [1992b]. On average case complexity of problems that are intractable in the worst case. *Pages 265–269 of: Proceedings of the 1992 American Control Conference*. Piscataway, NJ: IEEE Press.

Wasilkowski, G. W. [1992c]. On average complexity of global optimization problems. *Math. Programming*, **57**(2 (Ser. B)), 313–324.

Wasilkowski, G. W. [1993]. Integration and approximation of multivariate functions: average case complexity with isotropic Wiener measure. *Bull. Amer. Math. Soc.*, **28**, 308–314. Full version in *J. Approx. Theory*, **77**(2), 212–227.

Wasilkowski, G. W. [1996]. Average case complexity of multivariate integration and function approximation; an overview. *J. Complexity*, **12**, 252–272.

Wasilkowski, G. W. & Gao, F. [1992]. On the power of adaptive information for functions with singularities. *Math. Comp.*, **58**, 285–304.

Wasilkowski, G. W. & Woźniakowski, H. [1986]. Average case optimal algorithms in Hilbert spaces. *J. Approx. Theory*, **47**, 17–25.

Wasilkowski, G. W. & Woźniakowski, H. [1988]. On optimal algorithms in an asymptotic model with Gaussian measure. *SIAM J. Math. Anal.*, **3**, 632–647.

Wasilkowski, G. W. & Woźniakowski, H. [1989]. Mixed settings for linear problems. *J. Complexity*, **5**, 457–465.

Wasilkowski, G. W. & Woźniakowski, H. [1993]. There exists a linear problem with infinite combinatory complexity. *J. Complexity*, 326–337.

Wasilkowski, G. W. & Woźniakowski, H. [1994]. On strong tractability of multivariate problems. *Pages 621–628 of: Proceedings of IFIP '94*.

Wasilkowski, G. W. & Woźniakowski, H. [1995]. Explicit cost bounds of algorithms for multivariate tensor product problems. *J. Complexity*, **11**, 1–56.

Wasilkowski, G. W. & Woźniakowski, H. [1996]. On tractability of path integration. *J. Math. Phys.*, **37**(4), 2071–2088.

Wasilkowski, G. W. & Woźniakowski, H. [1997]. The exponent of discrepancy is at most 1.4778.... *Math. Comp.*, **66**, 1125–1132.

Weihrauch, K. [1987]. *Computability*. New York: Springer-Verlag.

Weiss, N., Wasilkowski, G. W., Woźniakowski, H., & Shub, M. [1986]. Average condition number for solving linear equations. *Linear Algebra Appl.*, **83**, 79–102.

Werschulz, A. G. [1987a]. An information-based approach to ill-posed problems. *J. Complexity*, **3**, 270–301.

Werschulz, A. G. [1987b]. What is the complexity of ill-posed problems? *Numer. Funct. Anal. Opt.*, **9**, 945–967.

Werschulz, A. G. [1989a]. Average case complexity of elliptic partial differential equations. *J. Complexity*, **5**, 306–330.

Werschulz, A. G. [1989b]. Information-based complexity and operator equations. *Pages 460–486 of: Mathematical Problems in Computation Theory*, vol. 21. Warsaw: Banach Center Publications.

Werschulz, A. G. [1989c]. Optimal algorithms for a problem of optimal control. *J. Complexity*, **5**, 144–181.

Werschulz, A. G. [1990]. Ill-posed problems in various settings: an information-based survey. *Pages 380–385 of: Proc. 1990 American*

Control Conference. Piscataway, NJ: IEEE Press.

Werschulz, A. G. [1991]. *The Computational Complexity of Differential and Integral Equations: An Information-Based Approach.* New York: Oxford University Press.

Werschulz, A. G. [1993]. The complexity of two-point boundary-value problems with analytic data. *J. Complexity,* **9,** 154–170.

Werschulz, A. G. [1994]. The complexity of two-point boundary-value problems with piecewise analytic data. *J. Complexity,* **10,** 367–383.

Werschulz, A. G. [1995a]. The complexity of multivariate elliptic problems with analytic data. *J. Complexity,* **11,** 154–173.

Werschulz, A. G. [1995b]. What is the complexity of solution-restricted operator equations? *J. Complexity,* **11,** 493–514.

Werschulz, A. G. [1996a]. The complexity of definite elliptic problems with noisy data. *J. Complexity,* **12,** 440–473.

Werschulz, A. G. [1996b]. The complexity of the Poisson problem for spaces of bounded mixed derivatives. *Pages 895–914 of:* Renegar, J., Shub, M., & Smale, S. (eds), *The Mathematics of Numerical Analysis.* Lectures in Applied Mathematics, vol. 32. Providence, RI: Amer. Math. Soc.

Werschulz, A. G. [1997]. The complexity of indefinite elliptic problems with noisy data. *J. Complexity,* **13,** 457–479.

Werschulz, A. G. & Woźniakowski, H. [1986]. Are linear algorithms always good for linear problems? *Aeq. Math.,* **31,** 202–211.

Winograd, S. [1967]. On the number of multiplications required to compute certain functions. *Proc. Nat. Acad. Sci.,* **58,** 1840–1842.

Woźniakowski, H. [1975]. Generalized information and maximal order of iteration for operator equations. *SIAM J. Numer. Anal.,* **12,** 121–135.

Woźniakowski, H. [1986]. Information-based complexity. *Pages 319–380 of: Annual Review of Computer Science,* vol. 1. Palo Alto, CA: Annual Reviews, Inc.

Woźniakowski, H. [1991]. Average case complexity of multivariate integration. *Bull. Amer. Math. Soc. (New Ser.),* **24**(1), 185–194.

Woźniakowski, H. [1992a]. Average case complexity of linear multivariate problems. I: theory. *J. Complexity,* **8,** 337–372.

Woźniakowski, H. [1992b]. Average case complexity of linear multivariate problems. II: applications. *J. Complexity,* **8,** 373–392.

Woźniakowski, H. [1992c]. Complexity of verification and computation for IBC problems. *J. Complexity,* **8,** 93–123.

Woźniakowski, H. (ed) [1993]. *Festschrift for Joseph F. Traub.* New York: Academic Press.

Woźniakowski, H. [1994a]. On tractability of linear multivariate problems (extended abstract). *Pages 212–236 of: Open Problems in Approximation Theory.* Bulgaria: Voneshta Voda.

Woźniakowski, H. [1994b]. Tractability and strong tractability of linear multivariate problems. *J. Complexity,* **10,** 96–128.

Woźniakowski, H. [1994c]. Tractability and strong tractability of multivariate tensor product problems. *J. Comput. Inform.,* **4,** 1–19.

Woźniakowski, H. [1994d]. Tractability of linear multivariate problems. *J. Complexity,* **10,** 96–128.

Woźniakowski, H. [1996a]. Complexity of multivariate problems with applications to path integrals. *Z. Angew. Math. Mech.,* **3,** 131–134. Presented at ICIAM/GAMM 95, July 3–7, 1995, Hamburg.

Woźniakowski, H. [1996b]. An introduction to information-based complexity. *Z. Angew. Math. Mech.*, **3**, 128–130. Presented at ICIAM/GAMM 95, July 3–7, 1995, Hamburg.

Woźniakowski, H. [1996c]. Overview of information-based complexity. *Pages 915–927 of:* Renegar, J., Shub, M., & Smale, S. (eds), *The Mathematics of Numerical Analysis*. Lectures in Applied Mathematics, vol. 32. Providence, RI: Amer. Math. Soc.

Woźniakowski, H. [1997a]. Computational complexity of continuous problems. *Pages 283–295 of:* Infeld, E., Zelazny, R., & Gałkowski, A. (eds), *Nonlinear Dynamics: Chaotic and Complex Systems*. Cambridge: Cambridge University Press.

Woźniakowski, H. [1997b]. Strong tractability of weighted tensor products. *Ann. Numer. Math.*, **4**, 607–622.

Xu, Z. B. & Shi, X. Z. [1992]. A comparison of point and ball iterations in the contractive mapping case. *Comp.*, **49**, 75–85.

Author index

Subject index

adaptive information, 11, 15
algorithm, 15
approximation problem, 28, 32, 36–38
average case setting, 6, 33–40

bounded noise, 89

cardinality number, 19
cardinality of information, 19
clock synchronization in distributed
    networks, 91
collateralized mortgage obligation, 24
combinatory complexity, 19
combinatory cost, 17
combinatory operations, 16
complexity, 3, 17
computability theory, 57
computational complexity, *see*
    complexity
contaminated information, 4
curse of dimensionality, 7, 27, 28, 91,
    107

discrepancy, 35, 44
discrete complexity, 28

entropy, 96–97
ε-approximation, 17
exponent of problem, *see* tractable,
    exponent

financial derivative, 47
FINDER software system, 49
fixed-point problem, 62
Fredholm problem of the second kind,
    62
function classes
    F_r, 25
    F_r^*, 26
    $\tilde{F}_r$, 37

Lipschitz, 12
functional integration, 53

Gaussian measure, 34
general formulation of IBC, 14–20
global information, 4, 11, 14
Gödel's theorem, 70–73

high-dimensional integration, 7, 43–52
history of IBC, 9, 105–107

IBC, *see* information-based complexity
ill-posed problems, 7, 57–60, 73
implementation testing, 8, 83–87
information, 3, 14
information complexity, 19
information cost, 16
information level, 6
information operator, 14, 15
information-based complexity, 5
integral equations, 28
integration, 6, 10–14, 21–23, 25–40,
    43–52, 88, 99
intractable, 8, 28, 70–73
intrinsic uncertainty, 5, 95

large linear systems, 100
linear programming, 8, 74–76
local information, 4, 11, 14
low discrepancy sequence, 46
    Faure, 46
    generalized Faure, 46
    generalized Niederreiter, 46
    Halton, 46
    Hammersley, 35, 46
    hyperbolic-cross, 36
    Sobol', 46

mathematical finance, 43–52
minimal radius of information, 30

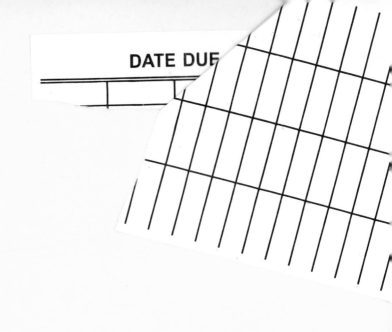

DATE DUE